The Gift

of an

Inner Moral Compass

Helping Our Children Grow Wise

Karyn Henley

Child Sensitive Communication

The Gift of an Inner Moral Compass
Helping Our Children Grow Wise

by Karyn Henley

Published by Child Sensitive Communication, LLC
Nashville, TN

Cover image: © shutterstock/Vitaliy Salo

ISBN 978-0-9986292-2-3 (prbk)
ISBN 978-0-9986292-3-0 (epub)
ISBN 978-0-9986292-4-7 (mobi)

www.KarynHenley.com

Table of Contents

Part One: Moral Wayfinding

Part Two: Practical Ways to Guide Children Toward Moral Wisdom

Part Three: Challenges

Part One:

Moral Wayfinding

Chapter 1
Where Do We Begin?

"Toto, . . . we're not in Kansas anymore."
– Dorothy in *The Wizard of Oz* film –

There were five neat rows, six wooden desks in each. Behind them, large windows showed a flat, treeless playground covered in stubbly grass. Fully stocked bookshelves lined the wall to the right. To the left hung a chalkboard and charts explaining antonyms, synonyms, and homonyms. At the front of the room, a map of China and the USSR had been pulled down like a window shade across the center chalkboard.

I was in sixth grade, and that map was the key to our assignment: memorize the rivers. This was during the Cold War, and we were afraid of a nuclear attack, so we practiced duck-and-cover drills at school. According to our teacher, being able to identify the rivers of China and the USSR would ensure that if we were ever captured and taken to Russia, we could follow the waterways to make our escape. I don't know if he was serious or if that was his ploy to get us to learn some geography, but we memorized the Volga, the Dneipr, the Yellow River, the Yangtze. We definitely wanted to be able to find our way home.

In a way, morality is about finding home. It's about having a compass that points True North so that wherever we are in life, we can orient ourselves and confidently head the right direction.

I recently read about a sport called orienteering. It's a type of cross-country race that involves finding your way. Writer Barbara O'Neal explains, "It is the sport of using a paper map and compass to find a series of flags as fast as possible. The long courses are expected to take the elite of the group about 40-50 minutes, which means a lot of people spend much longer running around a forest, off-trail, getting scratched by hostile plants and tumbling down hills . . ."[1] In other words, most of the contestants are *dis*oriented.

Sometimes it feels as if the whole world is disoriented, off kilter, out of balance. Of course, every age since the beginning of time has been out of balance in some way, but the present age may go down in the history books as one of the most unbalanced. Every day on any news station or site, we find reports about workplace harassment, sex abuse, domestic assaults, doping scandals, racial discrimination, bigotry, bullying, insensitivity to the needs of refugees and the poor, mass shootings . . .

Then there's the lack of moral leadership in the highest levels of government, where lying, deception, and corruption has taken root. We'd like to be able to point to our nation's leaders as examples of wisdom and morality. But many of them are just the opposite. We have to beware of "fake news" and "alternative facts," people calling truth falsehoods and falsehoods truth. Scandals erupt so head-spinningly fast that we get mentally dizzy trying to keep up with it all.

But believe it or not, there are a couple of bright spots in all this. First, this turmoil has brought morality into our daily conversations and is causing us to wrestle with the underbelly of our own lives, which we're usually adept at ignoring. Second, the fact that we're upset over it means we still have a conscience.

In 2011, twenty-nine men died at the Upper Big Branch mine, because Massey Energy repeatedly ignored safety standards. The company was ordered to pay a fine of millions of dollars. The sister of one of those miners said in a radio interview that the fine didn't begin to make up for the loss of twenty-nine miners. She said, "It's wrong on the very deepest level of morality." A second person said, "It's pretty easy to buy peace in this state."

When I heard that interview, I realized that the reason news reports reveal corruption is that these events, large or small, are an affront to our sense of what's right and good. The very fact that these stories are reported is proof that we know this is not the way things should be. The outcry tells us that people naturally understand that these things are wrong. Genocide, child abuse, murder – we humans know at a deep level that these are not right. We know there is a standard of accountability. That's obvious when we listen to news reports and hear people upset about injustice. "Look," we're saying, "This is wrong!" And sometimes, "How can we make this right? Who will take a stand?" Or better, "Here's what people are doing to turn this situation around."

It's the age-old good-versus-evil story, and as in Jesus's time, we religious are not immune to doing wrong ourselves and even doing it in the name of Christianity. A May 2018 Pew poll showed that the largest group opposing immigration into the United States is Christians – white evangelical Christians to be exact.[2] One reporter recently commented, "Some evangelicals are busy erasing bright lines and destroying moral landmarks."[3] We have a tendency to quickly brush aside these critiques, but when we ignore the mirror that's being held up to us, it's at our peril and our children's as well.

Have we slipped away from our moral mooring? Is our moral compass broken? Sometimes it feels as if we've lost our direction and no longer know how to locate True North. And yet . . .

In the supermarket recently, I saw a group of teenagers with Down Syndrome led by a teacher who was treating them so generously and graciously that I had to pause and watch and appreciate the whole group. Through "Room in the Inn," churches shelter the homeless on freezing winter nights. During the winter Olympics of 2018, one of the gold medal winners brought the silver and bronze winners up to stand next to him as equals on the podium. In the Parkland, Florida school shooting, teachers and students gave their lives to shield their friends. As Mr. Rogers advised, in times of trouble, "Look for the helpers. You will always find people who are helping."[4] In all nations, races, religions and walks of life, we will find them.

I come to the topic of morality and faith from a broad point of view, because I have a broad range of friends who are interested in the topic. I also come to it with a Christian slant, because I'm a Christian. But morality grows the same way in all people and gets stunted the same way in all people. Most of us are opposed to genocide, kidnaping, wartime atrocities, school shootings and massacres at concerts. Most of us believe that among humans, there is a basic level of moral decency that people should uphold. Most of us hold to some form of the Golden Rule, which was taught in the most ancient of civilizations and was recorded in the earliest religious writings.

We're concerned for our children and their future. How can we raise what researcher Robert Coles calls, "morally literate children"?[5] How can we guide them? How do we help them live wisely? What about the pervasive influence of screens? How can we help our children develop their God-given inner moral compass? Where do we begin?

The answer is that we begin at the beginning. "In the beginning, God created the heavens and the earth. . . God created man in his own image, in the image of God he created him; male and female he created them. . . God saw all that he had made, and it was very good" (Genesis 1:1, 27, 31). We begin with reverence and respect for what God created, from roses to rivers, from sparrows to stars, from fish to forests. We begin, too, with reverence and respect for people, for *imago dei*, the image of God in each person. God created, it is very good, and it's a serious matter to hurt, neglect, or damage what God made.

Yet we have that choice. And it's a moral one. Create or destroy. Help or hurt. Open our hearts or close them. It's amazing that God trusted us with earth, sky, sea, plants, animals, and each other. Such generosity. Such risk. Yet from the beginning, we humans were loved and entrusted with more gifts than we know what to do with. Including our children.

Neil Postman, educator and researcher on the role of media and culture, pointed out an obvious and weighty fact that we don't often consider: "Children are the living messages we send to a time we will not see."[6] Our parents could never have foreseen what our world is like now. We cannot foresee what our children's world will be like after we're gone. So how do we prepare them? It's hard enough to guide them through today much less anticipate what tomorrow might bring.

When we look at everything going on around us, we can either despair for our children's future or look forward with hope. I choose hope, because no matter what's happening in our world at the moment, there is – and always has been – a True North toward which a functioning moral compass points. We can teach our children how to use that compass. There is a guiding light for life, and we can help point the way.

Chapter 2
The Basic Elements of Wayfinding:
Values, Faith, and Morals

"Show me the way I should go, for to you I lift up my soul."
– Psalm 143:8 –

When it comes to making our way in life, few things are more important than our values, our faith, and our morals. These three influence our choices and determine the paths we take. So how do values, faith, and morals develop? We'll take a look at the stages of development in the next few chapters. But first, let's explore some terms. What are *values*? What exactly is *faith*? What do we mean by *morals*?

Several years ago, I spent a few weeks training Sunday School teachers in Kenya. On the first day of class, as I was greeting the teachers, one of them leaned in as he shook my hand and said, "We are a Christian nation. But, you see, there are Christians and there are *Christians*. You understand." And I did. He was saying that many people called themselves Christians but did not live like followers of Christ. The fact is, even though Kenya is considered a Christian nation, it's listed among the most corrupt nations in the world. So is a person a Christian or a *Christian*? It all boils down to what their values are.

Values

Robert Coles, in *The Moral Intelligence of Children*, wrote, "It is one thing to lay claim to values, to espouse them, and quite another to try to live them out, enact them over time with others."¹ It's not always easy to reconcile what we claim as our values with what we actually do and how we actually live. Claiming one set of values and living another is an age-old challenge that Jesus addressed. His harshest words were addressed to leaders who were not who they professed to be. "Woe to you, teachers of the law and Pharisees, you hypocrites!" he said. "You are like whitewashed tombs, which look beautiful on the outside but on the inside are full of dead men's bones and everything unclean. In the same way, on the outside you appear to people as righteous but on the inside you are full of hypocrisy and wickedness" (Matthew 23:28, 28, NIV). There was a mismatch between what they *claimed* as their values and what they actually valued.

We often talk about values as if they're simply a worldview, a set of ideals that represent perfection. But values are more down-to-earth than that. Simply put, our true values are . . . what we value. And what we value drives our choices. Values are revealed by what we do and say each day.

Our values often show up most clearly when we are under pressure. During the Y2K scare before 1999 turned into 2000, many of us worried that all the computers were going to malfunction because of the date change. Would we be able to buy food? Get gasoline? Access medical help? Many people, my family included, prepared for the worst by stocking up on non-perishable food, water, and medicines we might need. I envisioned the crisis bringing neighbors together to share whatever they had with whoever needed it. But then I heard a man at church claim that he was fortifying his home. He said he had a gun and would defend his family's stockpile of goods against anyone who might come for it. He was revealing his values.

Fortunately, the century changed without a hitch. Even now, I'm not sure any of us knows what we would have actually done if the crisis had materialized. But I suspect our true values would have been on full display.

Recently, as I watched news reports of people being evacuated from rapidly-spreading wildfires in California, I wondered: What if I had to escape my house as flames approached? I envisioned myself rushing out the door, knowing my house was in danger of burning to the ground. What would I have grabbed to take with me? Family and pets, of course, but what else? What do I value most? Phone. Meds. Irreplaceable photographs. Important papers and identity documents. A thumb drive containing records, backup files, or journal entries. I might grab a ring I inherited from my grandmother who died when I was twelve. I'd definitely try to take my computer, where so much of my writing and photos are stored.

What would *you* grab? What do you value so much that you would put it on your rescue list? Until we find ourselves in such a pressured situation, I'm not sure we can say exactly how we would respond. I suspect that we would discover what we truly care most about.

Barring disaster, there's a simpler way to find out what I value most. I can look at my credit card statements, the entries in my checkbook, and my budget history. How much did I spend? For what? Where? Why? And what's on my calendar? Where do I spend my time, money, and energy – physical and mental? My calendar shows what I value. If I say I value family but spend no time with family, then either I'm not being honest, or I'm struggling to overcome some obstacle that's keeping me from living out my true values.

Faith

Our values are inextricably linked to our faith, because faith is all about what we consider to be of *ultimate* value in life. The Christian's go-to scripture to define faith is usually Hebrews 11:1. The Marshall translation of the original Greek puts it this way: "Now faith is the reality of things being hoped, the proof of things not being seen." I've always found that verse – in any translation – to be a hard one to fully comprehend in a practical way. I think that's because it's not really a definition of faith but a description of one way that faith functions.

So how does faith function? The word *reality* in Hebrews 11:1 is a translation of the Greek word *hypostasis*, which literally means "that which supports from below." Faith functions as a support for our higher nature (our *imago dei*), for our hopes and dreams. Faith also functions as proof that what we value most is unseen: love, joy, peace, patience, kindness, goodness, faithfulness, balance, self-control, grace, mercy . . . in short, God. Faith is:

> – our spiritual attitude toward what we *value* most in life.
> – our viewpoint about what we consider to be life's
>   ultimate purpose and meaning.

– the inner spiritual orientation that governs our lives.

Since everyone is made in the image of God, everyone has a place – a space – in their souls for God. That means everyone has a faith of some sort, an inner spiritual attitude toward what they value most and what they consider to be life's ultimate purpose and meaning. Faith is part of each human being simply because of *imago dei* in each person. Since we humans are alive and changing, faith is alive and changeable. Faith ranges from weak to strong, stunted to growing, stagnant to fresh, shrunken to full, blind to open-eyed. We can welcome faith or deny it. We can nurture it or ignore it. Either way, it's an essential part of our being. So when we talk about "coming to faith," we're not talking about a one-time event but a process. Faith is not an end-point but a state of being, full of beginnings and possibilities. It's not boxed and finite but unboxed and infinite.

We often mask the true nature of faith by using the word *faith* when we really mean *belief.* The dictionary does say that both faith and belief can refer to trust and confidence, but there are important differences between the two words. My beliefs affect my faith, but my faith is not simply the sum of my beliefs. Neither are my beliefs the whole of my faith.

Beliefs are claims that we accept as true. They may or may not be true, they may or may not be based on proof, and, like faith, they may or may not relate to anything spiritual. What's more, beliefs can be listed and codified, and they often are. Beliefs can be mental or visceral, of the intellect or the gut. Where beliefs are concerned, we can choose to let someone else do the thinking for us. All we have to do is buy in.

But faith is different. It's as alive as our spirits. It's active. No one can do faith for us. As comparative religionist Wilfred Cantwell Smith says, belief is simply "the holding of certain ideas" while faith is "a quality of human living."[2] Beliefs are the docks we build out into the river; faith is the river. We can tear down docks, move them, or build new ones without draining the river, just as we can change our beliefs without losing our faith. The opposite is true as well. The river can change course and leave docks high and dry, just as a living, growing faith can change course, leaving blind beliefs behind. As many people have discovered, it's possible for a change of beliefs to broaden, deepen, and strengthen faith.

Morals

If faith is our spiritual attitude toward what we value most in life, then morality is our faith on display. "But someone will say, 'You have faith and I have works,'" wrote James. "Show me your faith apart from your works, and I by my works will show you my faith" (James 2:18). Morality is the way we live out our faith. It shows up in how we interact with people and how we treat our environment.

Basically, morality is respect, which comes from the Latin word *respectus* and means "the act of looking back." (Its root *specere*, "to look at," is where we get our word *spy*.) *Respect* means to give attention to, "to consider worthy of high regard, to esteem." Michele Borba, in her book *Building Moral Intelligence*, says, "Civility and common courtesy are traditional hallmarks of respect."[3] Notice too that civility and common courtesy are ways of acting and speaking. Morality is active, not passive. It's not simply claiming a set of beliefs or assenting to a certain lifestyle; it's a way of actually living from day to day.

The psychologists Jean Piaget, Lawrence Kohlberg, and John C. Gibbs speculated that, like the principles of math, the fundamental principles of morality are cosmic, built into the way the world works. In their research, they call basic morality "Ideal Normative Reciprocity," which simply means a balance in relationship, treating each other as respected equals.[4] In other words, it's the Golden Rule: "Do unto others as you would have them do unto you" (Matthew 7:12, Luke 6:31). Since ancient times, most religions have taught some form of the Golden Rule. Plato taught it around 350 BCE, long before Jesus's time: "[M]ay I be of a sound mind, and do to others as I would that they should do to me."[5]

As the Golden Rule indicates, respect is intended to be mutual. Reciprocal. In reality, as someone recently pointed out, people in positions of power, authority, or influence often think of respect as "respect my authority." But people who are not in power, who have little influence, or who are marginalized in some way often view respect differently. They, too, want respect, but to them, respect means "respect my humanity." That second viewpoint is what morality is about: respecting the humanity of every person. All of us deserve a basic level of respect and honor simply because we are all created in God's image.

We're born into the world with a feel for morality, but it's lopsided, focused only on one side of the Golden Rule equation: getting others to treat us as we want to be treated. For infants and young children, that self-centered focus is totally normal. But for an adult, that self-centered focus is totally immoral. So between infancy and adulthood, we need to accumulate some moral wisdom.

Like growing in faith, becoming morally wise is a lifelong process that we'll explore in the next few chapters as we look at an overview of the stages of mental, emotional, spiritual, and moral growth in children and teens. I've covered some of this in my book *Child-Sensitive Teaching*, which focuses on faith development and teaching tips for the Sunday School classroom.[6] Since this book focuses on moral development, after a brief look at the stages of growth, we'll explore specifics about morality, and we'll consider ways to help children grow morally wise.

As our framework, we'll use the psychosocial stages developed by Erik Erikson, along with cognitive research from Jean Piaget. In the area of morality development, we'll draw from the research of Lawrence Kohlberg, Martin Hoffman, and John C. Gibbs. In faith development, we'll primarily use the research of James Fowler.

As we explore the developmental stages, there are a couple of matters to keep in mind. First, these stages are a general guide. While all children go through all the stages in order, individual children mature at different rates, some maturing earlier than the average, some later. If children mature early, that does not mean they're extra intelligent. If they develop later, that does not mean they're deficient. It simply means they're growing at their own rate, as everyone does.

Second, I'll often use the term *significant adult*, so I want to clarify what I mean. Chances are, if you're reading this, you are one. So what do I mean by *significant adult*?

Significant adults are influencers. They influence a child's choices, which means they influence that child's future. Traditionally, the most significant adults in a child's life are Mom and Dad. But not always. Of course, parents will always have a significant impact on their children, even if one or both parents are missing. But while the absence of a parent is significant, when I use that term, I'm referring to adults who are present in the child's life, who play an active role, and who strongly influence the child's choices and values.

To discover who the significant people are for a particular child, ask, "Who spends time with the child? (Not just in the same house, but *with* the child.) Who listens to the child? Who plays with the child?" The answer to these questions will usually reveal the identity of the significant people in the child's life. (And they may not always be adults.)

Significant adults help children recognize and calibrate their moral compass. Novelist Scott Spencer, during a radio interview, said that one of his novels was inspired by the question, "What do you do when you are physically away from your moorings?" The answer, he explained, depends on your moral compass. His interviewer commented, "People close to us are our memory banks. They help explain our lives to us."[7] In a child's life, these people are the *significant adults*.

Being a significant adult is a great privilege. We are a memory bank – for the world, for our peers, and for our children. It's our job to show our children how to work with their own temperament and skills to navigate the world. We can help them find and use their inner moral compass and grow morally wise. How? That's what we'll explore in the second half of this book.

Several years ago, I met once a week for a Bible study with a friend who was a new Christian. One evening we were reading through one of Paul's letters, when she paused, sighed, and said, "I wish he had just listed the rules."

I've felt that way myself. Wouldn't it be easier to simply have a checklist of rules? Yes, just as it's easier to paint by number than to create an original piece of artwork. But life is not paint-by-numbers. Each life is an original work of art. We continually learn, experience, and discover. And because our faith and morals are an integral part of us, as we grow, they grow. As a consequence, we have to recalibrate our moral compass from time to time so that it reliably points the right direction. And there *is* a right direction. In morality as in wayfinding, there *is* a True North.

Chapter 3
Infants: Birth to Two
Trust vs. Mistrust

"We do not develop into the image of God;
we *are* the image of God."
– James R. Estep, Jr., *Christian Formation* –

<u>Emotional Growth</u>

We probably change more during our first two years
than at any other time of life. An infant goes from lying prone to
turning over to sitting up; from drinking only liquid to eating
solid food; from cooing to babbling to speaking understandable
words. But according to researcher Erik Erikson, one task
underlies all these changes: *trust.*[1] The challenge for the infant is
to learn to trust. Since trust is a foundation of our relationship
with God, the earliest years of life start the process of faith
development and set the stage for how that faith will grow.

How do infants learn to trust? It's really very simple.
Their caregivers consistently respond to them and take care of
their needs. At first, infants are completely dependent on others
for care, so the way their world interacts with them
communicates whether or not they can trust. When they're
hungry, are they fed? When they're cold, does someone wrap a

blanket or sweater around them? When their diaper is wet, are they given a clean, dry one?

Another factor in building trust is learning that when caregivers are out of sight, they are not permanently gone. They'll come back. Maybe Mom or Dad has simply left the room for a few minutes. Or they've gone to work for an entire day. Every time they return to their child, they strengthen trust.

Of course, there are times when even the best parents and caregivers fail to respond to the infant's needs. Fortunately, we don't have to be perfect. We just need to do the best we can to give consistent love and care. For the infant, as long as the scale is tipped solidly in favor of the positive – *trust* – then the strength of *hope* will emerge from this stage.

Hope is the belief that life will get better and all will be well. If children are consistently cared for – fed, cleaned, clothed, held, and loved – then they can be fairly certain that even in moments when they're cold, hungry, wet, uncomfortable, or even hurting, someone will take care of them. They can assume that they'll get what they need, and everything will turn out all right. They have hope.

If infants are neglected or abused, they learn just the opposite. Maybe they were abandoned. Or due to war or famine or other disasters, they were left needy. Or maybe there was often a change of caregivers. Then children learn that they can't trust anyone to take care of them. They grow to see people as unreliable and the world as unpredictable. As a result, they develop distrust. There's a crack in the foundation of their faith. Instead of carrying a strength into the next stage, they carry a weakness: insecurity – or at the extreme, hopelessness.

Mental Growth

Infants experience their world in the present moment, in the now. Their "classroom" is the tangible, sensory environment right in front of them – what they can see, hear, smell, touch, and taste at any given moment. The researcher Piaget called this a "sensorimotor" stage, which simply means that infants use their senses and their developing motor skills to explore and discover the world around them.[2] Learning comes naturally, and mental growth begins immediately. Everything is new. Every interaction is a discovery.

Spiritual Growth

James Fowler, a researcher who authored a classic study of faith development, labeled infancy as a stage of "undifferentiated faith,"[3] which means that the beginnings of spiritual sensitivity (trust, courage, hope, love) are not experienced as separate and distinct feelings but are lumped into one feeling: good. In simple terms, the infant discerns a very basic sense of good and bad, pain and pleasure, trust and mistrust.

At this point, these feelings are not attached to any idea of the divine but are part of the physical, sensory world of the infant's experience. Infants don't know the words *God* or *care* or *love*. In fact, they can't know those words in the abstract. But they do know the feeling of being loved and cared for. Or they know how it feels to lack care and love. That's the thing about the spiritual: It's not neutral. If we don't have care and love, we miss it. It becomes an emptiness. A lack. A need.

Moral Growth

Infants are born already having the internal capacity and sensibility for the development of an inner moral compass. But they are also born completely egocentric, which is the lowest stage of morality. That does not mean infants are making poor moral choices; it simply means they're not making conscious moral choices at all. According to Piaget, infants are in a pre-moral stage. They express their own wants and needs, demanding attention without regard for the wants and needs of others (like Mom, who needs a good night of sleep). But that's because infants are not yet capable of seeing the world from anyone else's perspective, so they don't understand that other people have needs too. In fact, at first an infant seems to consider her primary caregiver to be an extension of herself.

Still, the stepping stones of moral thinking are being laid even in infancy, first with the basic feelings of comfort and discomfort, pleasure and pain. Even more important is the awareness of a caregiver's acceptance or rejection. Since respect for others is the foundation of morality, when infants feel accepted and respected, they are on the way to accepting and respecting others. Conversely, when infants feel rejected, they are on the way to rejecting others.

The goal of moral development is empathy, according to theorist Martin Hoffman.[4] But empathy is slow to develop. We may think that newborns have an innate sense of empathy, because they cry when they hear other babies cry. The truth is, their response is egocentric. They are not empathizing with the other babies but cry simply because hearing others cry makes them feel distressed. Even a six-month-old in the presence of a distressed person will try to comfort *herself* by sucking her thumb or clinging to her mother or asking to be picked up. By the time she's one year old, she will try to comfort the distressed person. But why? Because the other person is upsetting *her*.

A basic requirement for the growth of morality is understanding cause and effect. We have to understand that our actions have consequences, that what we say and do affects other people. Infants are constantly learning cause and effect. They discover that they can bring smiles and frowns to the people around them. They also learn that their actions can elicit a "yes" or a "no."

Infants are sensitive to their caregiver's tone of voice and body language, which indicate approval and disapproval. Young children depend on these outward cues to guide them toward right choices. But moral development is a process, and children don't correctly discern between right and wrong *consistently* until they're about six years old.

Birth to Two

- egocentric
- premoral
- undifferentiated faith
- sensorimotor interaction with the world

Conflict: Trust vs. Mistrust
Strength: Hope

Chapter 4
Early Childhood: Twos and Threes
Autonomy vs. Shame

"Playing as children means
playing is the most serious thing in the world."
– G.K. Chesterton –

Emotional Growth

According to Erikson, children who are two and three years old are developing either *autonomy* or *shame*. An autonomous person is one who rules himself, which is exactly what two- and three-year-olds seem to want. They are beginning the process of becoming independent from their caregivers in order to establish their own unique identities. Of course, the search for identity can be a lifelong pursuit, but this is where it begins.

If you've ever been around a two- or three-year-old, you know that they usually push the limits of autonomy. They want to do things for themselves. Caregivers who recognize this as normal and beneficial will encourage toddlers to take on age-appropriate tasks like brushing their teeth, washing their face, and picking up toys. As toddlers learn to be independent in these small ways, they develop a sense of autonomy.

Of course, there are many things young children are not capable of doing, as well as many things that are too dangerous. So developing a healthy sense of autonomy can't depend on letting children do whatever they want. Instead, the key to autonomy is the attitude of the caregiver. When the child needs help, does the caregiver step in with criticism or encouragement? If children are not allowed to do simple tasks that they're perfectly capable of doing, or if their attempts are met with criticism and judgment, they develop a sense of shame. According to Erikson, shame is a feeling of being exposed. In this case, children feel that what has been exposed is their own deficiency and inadequacy.

If the scale is tipped in favor of autonomy, then children leave this stage with a strength that Erikson calls *will*, which is an appropriate description of twos and threes. We often call them strong-willed. And while we may moan about how difficult it is to go head to head with a two-year-old, in a few years that child may need the strength of will to stand up to peer pressure. To develop our identities, we have to develop our wills, and this stage is where *will* stakes its claim in no uncertain terms.

Mental Growth

Early childhood marks the beginning of what Piaget called the "preoperational" stage, which lasts until the child is about seven years old. (Some experts believe that Piaget's stages are too rigid, but they work for our general purposes here.) *Operation* is Piaget's way of describing a thought process that allows a child "to do in his mind what before was done physically." Adult-like, logical reasoning is operational. So *preoperational* means that, at this stage, a child is not able to reason with adult-like logic.

This doesn't mean that young children aren't logical. It simply means that they think with childlike logic. One three-year-old exclaimed, "Mommy, I know why they call it the moon! Because the cow jumped over it and said, MOOO!" Young children also tend to think literally. (Mom lost her voice – where did she lose it? Maybe I can find it for her.) And young children don't understand the flow of time. "A long time ago" was yesterday at Grandma's house. If you tell a young child, "Your birthday is only two weeks away," he may wake up tomorrow morning and ask, "Is it my birthday yet?"

Twos and threes still see themselves as the center of their universe as they try to make sense of the outside world, which from their viewpoint, revolves around them and their everyday activities. They move through their world like a whirlwind, constantly learning through their five senses. To find out how they affect the world, they perform simple cause and effect experiments: What will happen if I push this button, pull this string, or take that apart? All this exploring keeps their caregivers hopping.

Spiritual Growth

If children are taught to believe in God, this is the stage when they begin to form ideas and images of what they think God is like. Often these images have human characteristics. I call this the "fantasy/imitative" stage, based on Fowler's description of this stage as "the fantasy-filled, imitative phase in which the child can be powerfully and permanently influenced by examples, moods, actions and stories" of the significant adults in their life. This stage of faith lasts until children are about six or seven.

Fowler emphasizes the adult's tremendous responsibility at this stage. He says, "The imagination and fantasy life of a child can be exploited by witting or unwitting adults." Religious stories, images, and symbols that adults share with children "can prove life-opening and sustaining of love, faith and courage" or give rise "to fear, rigidity and the brutalization of souls."[1] That's because young children generally believe what they are told without questioning whether or not it's true. If they're told there's a Santa Claus or an Easter bunny or a tooth fairy, they believe it. They still have difficulty distinguishing between fantasy and reality, and imagination plays a big role in their lives.

Think of all the religious stories and concepts young children are taught. They don't question or weigh what's true or untrue but believe what they're told, just as they believe in Santa Claus. They assume that adults are telling the truth, which means that young children have a taken-for-granted faith.

That's the "fantasy" related part of this stage. What about the "imitative"? Young children cannot enter the adult world, so they imitate significant adults, mimicking the outward expressions of adult faith that they've witnessed – religious forms, practices, rites, and rituals. That includes the way adults incorporate their faith into their daily lives.

Moral Growth

As Erikson pointed out, *will* is the strength that should develop at this stage. That's both good news and challenging news. It's good news because it's a sign that toddlers are maturing. It's challenging news because it means they are now aware that they can make deliberate choices. With deliberate choices come moral decisions: Do I assert my will or submit my will? Everyone in a toddler's world is drawn into the child's struggle to find the balance.

For toddlers, the struggle with will is intensely difficult. Even though they're maturing, they're still quite egocentric, so everything in the world is theirs to see, smell, taste, touch, or hear. Everything is potentially "mine." The way young children play reflects this struggle. Twos and threes engage in what's called "parallel play," which means they play side by side but not cooperatively together. Two toddlers may be playing with blocks beside each other, but "these are mine and those are yours" and never the twain shall meet. If I decide one of yours is mine, we have a big problem.

The good news is that as children approach age three, they reach a developmental milestone: They begin "perspective taking." This means that toddlers *begin* to be able to understand another person's viewpoint and realize that other people have rights, opinions, possessions, and feelings just the way they do.

One two-year-old girl, who was not yet at the perspective-taking stage, hit a boy in her play group. Her mother, appalled, asked her, "How do you think that felt?" The little girl studied her fist and answered, "It felt pretty good." She interpreted even Mom's question egocentrically.

Dr. Thomas Lickona, who has studied developing morality, has a wonderfully concise way of explaining these stages: "What's right" to a child at this stage, says Lickona, is "to get my own way."[2] This is stage one of morality, according to researchers. It's what we might call "superficial" morality, in which the reason to be "good" is to gain reward and/or avoid punishment. (Note: It's possible for older kids and even adults to revert to - or live in - this egocentric stage, in which "what's right is to get my own way.")

With superficial morality, children depend on consistently enforced rules to help them discern what's right and what's wrong. Consistent rules also give children a sense of safety and security. They may buck the rules, but having no rules - or having rules that are inadequate or inconsistently enforced - leaves children feeling uncertain, insecure, and anxious.

One thing about toddlers: They usually have to be told the same rules over and over again. It's hard for them to generalize and understand that a rule may apply everywhere and in all situations. In other words, if a child is told to share at Timmy's house, he takes that directive as specific and limited (at Timmy's house), not as a general rule (*always* share your toys). So with a change of playmate or location, children may have to hear the directive again.

Respecting other people includes people of other cultures and races. Dr. Marguerite Wright researches racial awareness in children. She calls the stage from birth to age three a time of "racial innocence."[3] Children of this age see people as individuals, not as groups. In fact, until they're about five years old, children don't see people as members of any kind of group – unless adults point that out. We are not born with bias. It's the significant people in our lives who influence our first thoughts about race, ethnicity, gender, religion, and socioeconomic status. It's the significant people in our lives who first calibrate our moral compass.

Two and Three

- fantasy/reality confusion
- strong imagination
- impressionable, gullible
- imitating significant adults
- childlike logic, literal thinking
- developing a "sense of other"
- rule dependent

Conflict: Autonomy vs. Shame
Strength: Will

Chapter 5
Early Childhood: Fours and Fives
Initiative vs. Guilt

"The answers aren't important really . . .
What's important is - knowing all the questions."
- Zilpha Keatley Snyder, *The Changeling* -

Emotional Growth

The next life crisis, according to Erikson, is the struggle between initiative and guilt. People with initiative do things without being asked. They're assertive, think independently, and are what we would call self-starters. That's a good description of most children at four and five years old. They're little scientists, trying to impose order on their rapidly expanding world. They're out to explore, examine, and discover. Eager to learn and know, they ask hundreds of questions a day, some so off-the-wall that they have no real logical answer, others quite deep, like my son's "Why does the skin on your body never end?"

When children's natural inclination to explore is encouraged, they develop a sense of initiative. Of course, four and five year olds are limited by what they are capable of doing and by what may be inappropriate or dangerous. Even so, initiative can develop if caregivers respond respectfully, affirming the child's impulse to explore and discover. On the other hand, if children are ridiculed or continually restricted and told that they're not capable, they begin to feel guilty for their natural curiosity and their urge to explore.

If children develop their sense of initiative, the strength that emerges is called *purpose*. They sense that there's a purpose for their curiosity and questions, a purpose for the order of nature and the world around them, and perhaps most important, a purpose for them in the world.

Mental Growth

Fours and fives are still in the preoperational stage, and they still learn primarily through their five senses, but they're developing significant mental skills. One of the most important of these skills, according to researcher Howard Gardner, is the ability to understand and work with symbols.[1] Because fours and fives are just beginning this growth, they still often think literally and with childlike logic. One father reported that he and his four-year-old son were walking down a flight of stairs, when the boy suddenly stopped and exclaimed, "I know why we have cracks in our bottoms! It's so we can go down the stairs!" Another preschooler saw a house being moved on the flat bed of a truck. "That house must have been really dirty," he said. "They had to lift it up to sweep all the dirt out from under it." Which is logical. From a child's point of view.

Fours and fives are proud of their age and may announce it to anyone they meet. They are now aware that they're growing, getting older, better, smarter, and stronger. This focus on age may also have to do with their growing interest in numbers and counting. They seem to want to count everything, which correlates to their growing ability to make and use symbols.

Because exploration and discovery are so much a part of their lives, fours and fives are more aware of what's happening in the world around them. By five, they're also beginning to recognize the difference between fantasy and reality. But there's still a lot they don't understand, so they may develop fears they haven't had before. They want and need understanding and comfort. Again, they can easily be made to feel guilty, not only for what they do and say but also for what they want and feel.

Spiritual Growth

Four and five year olds are still in the fantasy-imitative stage of faith that began around age two. They live what they imagine and imitate the visible signs of faith that they witness in the significant adults in their lives. As in the previous stage, young children believe whatever they're told. That's why we often idealize the "pure" faith of children. They take their faith for granted and don't question it. In other words, "that's just the way it is," and that's perfectly normal for this stage.

Moral Growth

At about age five, children move up to a new level of morality. They have a better understanding of the concept of consequences – cause and effect, if/then. They know they can be the cause of positive effects or negative effects. They can cause someone to laugh or to cry, and they generally know which one they're supposed to do. According to Dr. Lickona, they would define "right" as "doing what I'm told."

Children in this stage still depend on rules to guide them in knowing and choosing what's right, and they ask themselves whether they'll be rewarded or punished for doing whatever they're considering. The big question is, "Will I get in trouble if I do this?" In Kohlberg's model of moral development, this stage is characterized by the avoidance of punishment.[2]

The good news is that by this stage children have internalized much of the teaching and training they received in earlier years, and that training is now forming their conscience. If they've been taught to respect others, then they know it's wrong to take toys from other children, it's right to share, it's wrong to hit, it's right to help, and so on. Dr. Robert Solomon, a professor of philosophy, points out that the conscience is, in many ways, the sensibility of "being caught in the act." In essence, we "catch ourselves." That's what moral education does for us. We learn to control ourselves. As Dr. Solomon says, "Our own self-consciousness imposes the internal judgment."[3]

Of course, children don't always go by what their developing consciences tell them (and neither do we adults). They share selectively, picking and choosing what to share and when, and they still have trouble seeing from any viewpoint but their own. So they continue to need external help to confirm when they are on the right or wrong track.

This new level of morality is reflected in the way four and five year olds play. Instead of playing "parallel" (side by side but not together) like toddlers do, fours and fives engage in "associative play." That means they interact cooperatively with other children. "You be the mommy, and I'll be the baby." Or "You be the store man, and I'll come buy some ice cream." Or "You make the road with the blocks, and I'll drive my car over it." This type of interaction requires a level of respect for the other person that indicates a higher level of morality.

With this higher level of morality comes an increasing ability to empathize emotionally with others. Empathy is an important characteristic of a moral person. In the previous stage, it began to develop as perspective-taking, the realization that other people have feelings and opinions and possessions. Now it grows into empathy as children actually begin to understand and be sensitive to the feelings and experiences of others.

Fours and fives also begin *identifying* with the values of the significant people in their lives. A five-year-old may report with shock, "Did you hear the word *he* said?!" Or "Do you know what movie *they're* going to watch tonight?!" Four- and five-year-olds are discovering that not all people share the same values. As for them? They identify with the values of significant adults and use those values as a guide.

To young children, there are no moral nuances. They think in terms of all or nothing. Everything is either bad or good, wrong or right, acceptable or unacceptable, safe or dangerous. There's nothing in between.

As far as racial awareness goes, Dr. Marguerite Wright has found that children between three and five are becoming aware that people have different skin color, but she says that this awareness comes without prejudice. It's perceived on the same level as wearing different clothes, says Michele Borba, in

Building Moral Intelligence.[4] According to Dr. Wright, it's around age five that children begin to make distinctions in racial differences. But it's no big deal to them – unless significant adults make it a big deal.

Four and Five
- starting to sort out fantasy from reality
- strong imagination
- childlike logic, literal thinking
- no moral nuances
- rule dependent
- conscience developing
- identifying with values of significant adults

Conflict: Initiative vs. Guilt
Strength: Purpose

Chapter 6
Six Through Nine
Industry vs. Inferiority

"Two important things to teach a child:
to do and to do without."
– Marcelene Cox –

Emotional Growth

Erikson viewed this stage as a crucial time for creating either a sense of industry or inferiority. So what is industry? An industrious person is someone who is busy being productive, which accurately describes six- to nine-year-olds, who are mastering new skills and are eager to show their prowess. How fast can I run? How high can I jump? How far can I throw the ball? How many times can I skip rope without missing? How well can I knit or draw or make a bracelet? When children in this stage are encouraged in their efforts to be busy and productive, and when they discover where they can succeed, they develop a sense of industry.

Inferiority, the negative side of this stage, can develop in a variety of ways. Peers play a greater role now, and because kids want to fit into a group and belong, if they're bullied or rejected, they can easily feel inferior. The adults in a child's life play an important role too. If adults set goals that are too high and children can't live up to expectations, they feel inferior. This is especially true if they perceive that being loved and accepted depends on their performance and achievements. For children in that situation, the consequences of failure are enormous.

Inferiority can also result if an adult does the child's work for him. Adults know they can usually do projects faster and better than children, but when the adult takes over, it signals that "you're not capable; your work is not good enough." Or perhaps the adults don't take over, but neither do they allow children to practice their skills. Every time the child gets out glue and paint, the adult says, "Put that away; all you ever do is make a mess." Not that adults should allow chaos, but as with previous stages, there are respectful ways to respond that will encourage children and set limits at the same time.

At this stage, children want to know, "What do *I* do well?" Naturally competitive, they compare their abilities to what their classmates and friends are able to do. Adults can help by pointing out that people excel in different areas and by helping children recognize their gifts and strengths. We can give them a vision for who they are and what they can do. When children go through this stage developing the positive sense of industry, they reap a bonus: the strength of *competence* (built on the word *compete*). They feel capable. This powerful asset forms a strong foundation for future accomplishments.

Mental Growth

According to Piaget, six-year-olds are in their last year of moving from being pre-operational (reasoning with childlike logic) to being "concrete operational," a new stage that lasts through age eleven. In the concrete operational stage, children can reason with adult logic, but they do this best when they have something concrete on which to base their thinking. In other words, children are not usually ready for totally abstract thinking. In order to reason logically, they need to see or handle something concrete that is either physically present or physically represented.

More recent research has shown that in some areas, children reach this concrete operational stage earlier than Piaget thought. Researcher Howard Gardner believes a child can be preoperational in the area of language but concrete operational in the area of drawing or number.[1] This would account for why some children seem to understand symbolism, with concrete representations, in certain subject areas much earlier than age seven. Still, age seven is often known as "the age of reason." By then most children have moved from literal interpretations of words, events, and stories to an understanding of symbolism and deeper meanings.

At this stage, children are also able to perceive distance, time, and space more accurately. Because they better understand the flow of time, they begin studying events of history and can perceive those events chronologically. They also memorize more easily and are able to retain a lot of information. Age nine is sometimes called "the golden age of memory."

Spiritual Growth

Throughout this stage, children still have a taken-for-granted faith and generally continue to believe what they're taught about religion and spirituality. However, they also begin asking insightful and sometimes uncomfortable questions. One six-year-old asked, "Why is God a He, not a She?"

Fowler calls this the mythic-literal stage, because children's growing faith depends in large part on the stories they see and hear each day, especially stories told by significant adults. Fowler says that the child "begins to take on for him- or herself the stories, beliefs and observances that symbolize belonging to his or her community."

Moral Growth

Around age six, children begin to *consistently* discern correctly between right and wrong, although they still depend on rules to guide their behavior. From six to nine, they seem to have a strong, innate sense of justice and are alert to infractions of the rules. "It's not fair" is a common complaint, and they're quick to point a finger at anyone who breaks the rules. At this age, children have a fairness-focused "eye for an eye, tooth for a tooth" sense of morality. But they often have a double standard as well: Justice for all, mercy for me. Dr. Lickona says they believe "right" is to "look out for myself but be fair to those who are fair to me." Researchers call this stage of morality "concrete moral reciprocity."

Toward the end of this stage, children begin to transition from this tit-for-tat view of morality to a more altruistic view. They begin to realize that there's a sense of satisfaction in doing good deeds "for free," that is, without requiring that a good deed be done for them in return.

Children from age five to seven are "awakening to social color," says Dr. Wright. By age eight, they're aware of differences between races and are usually able to correctly identify most races. If the significant adults in children's lives welcome and include people of different races, children will too. If significant adults show racial prejudice, children will most likely show the same prejudice, although they may not fully understand what that means or what the consequences are.

Six Through Nine
- moving from literal to symbolic reasoning
- concrete operational
- competitive
- rule oriented
- story centered faith
- eye for eye morality

Conflict: Industry vs. Inferiority
Strength: Competence

Chapter 7
Tweens: Ten Through Twelve
Industry vs. Inferiority
and
Identity Formation vs. Identity Confusion

"The years between 10 and 14 are known as
the storm-and-stress period,
because so much change – physical, emotional, social –
can happen seemingly all at once."
– Sue Corbett –

Emotional Growth

Tweens are sandwiched in an awkward space between elementary age children and the youth of adolescence. I say awkward because they have a foot in each world and often seesaw back and forth. Some tweens definitely lean younger, toward childhood. Others already seem to be young teens. But most of them vacillate between child and teen, which is why we'll see some of the previous stage reflected in this chapter as well as previews of the coming stage of adolescence.

The biggest leap probably occurs between ten and eleven, which seems to be a transition period. Parents usually experience this transition as a decrease in communication. The door to the tween's bedroom, which was always open before, is now closed and may have a sign on it: "Private." Or "Knock Before Entering." Or even "Keep Out." In general, boys become more restless, and girls become moody. Many girls begin menstruating, although the average age for this is twelve and a half. The point is, tweens are moving into the world of emotional weather patterns we might call "hormonal disturbances." Thrown out of balance, they're uncertain and often uncomfortable with the changes they're experiencing.

Another factor that makes this stage awkward is that boys usually enter puberty later than girls. Of course, puberty comes later for some girls as well. Social groupings tend to mirror this uneven rate of maturity. In previous stages, boys and girls generally mixed spontaneously during activities, but now they tend to gather in separate groups. Among those of the same gender, those who mature earlier often flock together in cliques, leaving late-bloomers to form separate social groups.

As in the previous stage, tweens have the task of continuing to develop a sense of *industry*, but now we can add the task of *identity formation*. As we saw in the previous chapter, developing a sense of industry involves the child mastering skills and discovering abilities. This discovery becomes a foundation for the tween's growing search for identity, which will continue through the teen years.

The negative side of the equation is the sense of *inferiority* we discussed in connection with the previous stage. Add the growing self-consciousness of the tween, and we get the beginnings of teen angst that worries, "What do *they* think of me?" Still, tweens don't usually spend an inordinate amount

of time in self-reflection, at least not as much as they will in the
next stage.

The negative of identity formation is *identity confusion*,
which we'll discuss in more detail in the following chapter. For
now, it's important to note that if a tween is developing a sense
of industry and identity, the strength of *competence* should
continue to emerge, and the strength of *fidelity* should begin
developing. Fidelity is faithfulness – in this case, faithfulness to
who they are and what they stand for. Since adolescence is the
time in which the process of identity and fidelity formation
reaches its peak, we'll save that discussion for the following
chapter as well.

Mental Growth

The years between infancy and age five encompass the
fastest period of brain growth, but the tween stage is the second
fastest. "Brain changes during the early teen years set up four
qualities of our minds during adolescence: novelty seeking,
social engagement, increased emotional intensity, and creative
exploration," says Daniel J. Siegel, a professor of psychiatry at
UCLA.[1]

The passage from childhood into adolescence marks the
transition into the stage Piaget calls "formal operational," which
starts around age twelve. With formal operations, tweens begin
to be able to reason abstractly and with adult logic. One of the
welcome benefits of this brain growth is that tweens are able to
concentrate for longer stretches of time.

And there's more good news: This brain growth signals
a coming maturity that will bring the ability to maturely process

reality. The bad news is that it doesn't happen overnight but develops slowly over a fairly long period of time. Psychologist Daniel Goleman says, "The prefrontal-limbic neural circuitry crucial to the acquisition of social and emotional abilities is the last part of the human brain to become anatomically mature, a developmental task not completed until the mid-twenties."[2] So the tween stage is the beginning of a long haul.

When we looked at early childhood, we noted that children are not able to consistently tell the difference between fantasy and reality until they're about five years old. But one type of fantasy continues through the tween and even teen years. We know it as "wishful thinking." It goes something like this: "Me? I can drink beer and not get drunk." Or "I won't get pregnant." Or "I won't get an STD." "Those things may happen to other people, but not to me." For girls, this type of fantasy lasts until around the age of sixteen or seventeen. For boys, it lasts into their early twenties. So here again, when we discuss tweens, we find ourselves flowing right into the next stage.

Spiritual Growth

Tweens still have the story-centered faith of the previous stage. This includes the faith-related or spiritually significant stories told by their parents, their faith community, and their friends. It also includes their own personal stories as they experience – or don't experience – a connection with the spiritual.

One cultural factor that influences spiritual growth is pluralism. A pluralistic society is one in which each different ethnic, racial, religious, and social group keeps its own identity and culture within a common civilization. Our society is pluralistic, which means that children compare their spiritual beliefs with the beliefs of others. Tweens may begin questioning, challenging, perhaps even arguing with beliefs they have been taught, beliefs that until now, they have taken for granted.

Moral Growth

Tweens still have the rule-oriented, fairness-focused, double-standard morality that characterizes younger children, but they are shifting from Concrete Reciprocity (I'll be fair to whoever's fair to me) to Ideal Reciprocity (basically the Golden Rule: Treat others the way you want to be treated). Dr. Lickona says that they generally define "what's right" as "being nice so that others will think well of me and I can think well of myself." Tweens still tend to reason with payback logic – getting even or balancing the score.

Now that tweens are beginning to reason abstractly, moral issues become more complex. They're better at gauging right and wrong, but now they also see moral nuances, gray areas where right and wrong are not so easy to pin down: image vs. character, justice vs. mercy, friends vs. enemies vs. frenemies. But they're also getting better at thinking through social issues and suggesting solutions. As they mature, they become more sensitive to inconsistencies between what they've been taught and what they actually see and hear from the significant adults in their lives. They quickly pick up on hypocrisy, astutely seeing disparities between what adults say and what adults do.

On the other hand, tweens tend to be relationally shallow and self-serving. They may act or speak impulsively, not thinking about the consequences. As they grow through this stage, they often test limits and challenge boundaries that seem arbitrary to them. And their dilemmas become increasingly more teenlike.

Tweens tend to conform to the wishes of the significant people in their lives – the people who spend time with them, work and play with them, and really listen to them when they have something to say. The biggest influences on their values are media, peers, school, and parents.

Advertising and media focus a huge amount of attention on kids this age, who have become the perfect targets. One reason is that parents spend more money on tweens than on any other age group. A second reason is that tweens are growing more self-conscious, peer-conscious, and body-conscious. In other words, image-conscious. And that perfectly fits advertisers' goals, because they're hired to make consumers believe that purchasing and using certain products will enhance their image.

A third reason advertisers target tweens is that kids at this stage are moving rapidly toward the adolescent stage, in which they are developing their personal identity, deciding who they are or at least how they would like to be perceived. Product creators, sellers, and advertisers want their products and brands to become part of the young person's identity: "I'm a Pepsi guy." "I'm an Urban Outfitters kind of girl." The product-peddlers want to get a head start on claiming loyalty, so this age looks like

their perfect match. All of this advertising attention contributes
to the push and pull of the moral tug-of-war over values.

Ten Through Twelve
- one foot in childhood, one in adolescence
- rule oriented, fairness focused
- challenge boundaries
- story centered faith, questioning
- self-conscious, image-conscious
- peer and gender sensitive, forming groups

Conflict: Industry vs. Inferiority
and
Identity Formation vs. Identity Confusion
Strength: Competence and the beginning of Fidelity

Chapter 8
Adolescence:
Thirteen to Twenty
Identity Formation vs. Identity Confusion

"[T]he adolescent period of life is in reality
the one with the most power for courage and creativity."
– Daniel J. Siegel –

Emotional Growth

As teens mature year by year, they leave the awkwardness of the tween stage and enter young adulthood. This is the last stage of what began in infancy: becoming an independent person. It's no surprise, then, that the adolescent's main task is to develop a sense of *identity*. That search for identity, which began in the previous stage, now intensifies as teens try to figure out who they are, what they believe, and where they plan to go in life. They explore different roles available to them and choose a path to pursue for the future.

For this reason, adolescents continue to be targets for the marketing pitches of almost anyone and everyone who has a product to sell. In an in-depth look at marketing and the youth culture, commentator David Kupelian said that "teenagers increasingly look to the media to provide them with a ready-made identity predicated on today's version of what's cool."[1]

But, he pointed out, advertising and media are interested in promoting a *consumer* identity, not necessarily a *healthy* identity. In fact, part of the teen struggle centers on exactly what identity is and where to find it, because what's being sold as identity is really about *image.* True identity is based on *character* in the sense of personal integrity. Beliefs. Values. So in the identity search, teens often try ideas on for size. This sometimes leads them to express themselves strongly on issues in order to hear themselves take a stand that differs from the views of the adult(s) in the discussion. In essence, the teen is trying to prove what the two-year-old discovered so long ago: I am a person in my own right. I am not you.

Social media is another place teens establish their identity and exhibit their image. Anastasia Goodstein of Ypulse, an online site that covers youth marketing and research, said of social media, "Teens are narcissistic and exhibitionist. For teens, especially, who are going through this stage where they're constantly looking for that affirmation and validation and response for everything they are, it's addictive."[2] Media and advertising fit right in, since, "Brands are about giving you value, giving you self-esteem," says Juliet Schor in her book *Born to Buy.*[3] Image, identity, and marketing are all connected in the teen world.

Teens push against boundaries, and adults usually push back. Ideally as teens move through this stage, adults allow them to make more and more of their own decisions. With loving support and age-appropriate boundaries, teens are usually able to begin figuring out who they are and what they stand for. On the other hand, a sense of *identity confusion* may develop if a teen is still treated like a child, or if the teen's views and opinions are not heard or valued. This can also happen if someone maps out a teen's future path for them.

But if the scale is tipped in favor of the positive, and teens are growing into their own sense of identity, they emerge from this stage with the strength of *fidelity*. As noted in the previous stage, fidelity means *faithfulness* – in this case, fidelity simply means being faithful to their beliefs and values and being true to who they are.

Mental Growth

By now, the adolescent is solidly in the formal operational stage. This means that teens can think about thinking, which is something they couldn't do previously. They are also growing more adept at using adult logic and dealing with abstract concepts and hypothetical situations. However, many teens choose *not* to reason more maturely, or they use mature thinking sporadically, says Kevin Huggins, who spent years working with youth.[4] But why would a teen choose not to think maturely? Huggins says:

Teens may reason immaturely if they're under a lot of stress. When we're stressed, we tend to revert to more immature ways of thinking and acting. (Actually, that applies to anyone of any age.)

Teens may reason immaturely, because mature thinking grows out of pain, problems, and hardship, which is exactly what they try to avoid – and what we adults try to help them avoid. Parents contribute to immaturity by being overprotective and over-controlling in an effort to save their kids from . . . yes: pain, problems, and hardship.

Teens may reason immaturely, because one way mature thinking develops is by interacting with people who think maturely – specifically, older, wiser adults. Many young people spend more time with peers and less time with mature adults.

As teens' horizons broaden each year, they see a wider range of choices than they saw before. They also begin to realize that each choice comes with corresponding risks and rewards. What to do? Decision-making may become difficult, and whether the issue under consideration is mundane or critical, teens may be slow to actually make a choice. So while teens can be impulsive, they can also be indecisive, anxiously worrying and weighing their choices.

Another characteristic of teens is their tendency to exaggerate and respond with over-the-top reactions. They often contradict themselves. One moment a sixteen-year-old girl proclaims, "I can't stand chocolate." A short time later, she's saying, "Snickers! That's my favorite candy!"

Spiritual Growth

Because adolescents are trying to establish their identity, the teen years are a time to personalize their faith. Fowler says that in order to make faith personal and real, teens need to understand how faith relates to all the areas of life they're involved in: family, school, peers, work, media, church groups, hobbies, and other interests. Faith "must provide a basis for identity and outlook," he says, and must be able to function not only in the area of the unseen but also in the realm of practical interactions with the world.

This is a stage full of questions and tension. Teens do not want to simply imitate their parents' or friends' faith but want to develop strong beliefs of their own. They want to have their own values and their own faith. Teens, then, may rebel against their previous, taken-for-granted beliefs, not necessarily in the sense of revolting but in the sense of refusing to "buy in." This opens the way to personalizing their faith.

Moral Growth

Novelist Orson Scott Card wrote that the life of the adolescent is "full of passion, intensity, magic, and infinite possibility; but lacking responsibility, rarely expecting to have to stay and bear the consequences of error. Everything is played at twice the speed and twice the volume in the adolescent – the romantic – life."[5] That's a reminder of the "wishful thinking" type of fantasy that characterizes this stage, the "it won't happen to me" mindset. As I mentioned previously, that type of wishful thinking lasts until around sixteen or seventeen for girls and into the early twenties for boys.

As a result of formal reasoning, teens can think about what others might be thinking of them. They may also contemplate how different value systems would work in their life as they search for what "fits" them. As a result, they may set aside their parents' viewpoint, at least for a while, and try on another viewpoint instead.

Although teens are still in the stage of Ideal Reciprocity (the Golden Rule), they are able to look beyond the face value of an action to evaluate intentions, motives, social conditions, or life influences of the people responsible for the action. Their definition of what's right may also shift. "Right" may become "what's right for the group." But there's a flip side to reciprocity: Researcher John C. Gibbs points out that "reciprocity can serve many masters – including hate."

Since one of the teen's strongest desires is to be accepted, their morality tends to be conformist. When they have a moral decision to make, they often wonder, "What will *they* think of me if I do this (or if I don't do this)?" *They* are the people who are significant in the teen's life – maybe his peer group or a best friend. Being part of a peer group is appealing, because it confers teens with an automatic identity. But it also comes with a risk if they decide not to go along with group-think. They may have a hard time asserting their individual identity. Of course, parents, too, may continue to be significant influencers in a teen's life. Other relatives, teachers, and coaches may play a significant role as well.

Some young adults of high school and college age grow into an even more mature stage of morality in which they measure moral decisions by social norms or even in universal terms. Facing death in a traumatic event like a school shooting or a life-threatening illness can also give teens – and even tweens – a more mature perspective on morality. Also, teens who are more contemplative and principled in their age group often move into the more mature moral stages in which their morality is part of how they perceive themselves. It has already become part of their identity.

<u>Thirteen to Twenty</u>
- questioning and tension
- personalizing faith/spirituality
- adult reasoning
- alert to the expectations of others
- conformist morality

Conflict: Identity vs. Identity Confusion
Strength: Fidelity

Chapter 9
Morality: A Thumbnail Sketch

"The thorns which I have reaped are of the tree I planted."
    – Lord Byron –

Before we turn to practical ways to help children develop their inner moral compass, let's briefly trace the stages of moral development through childhood and into the more mature stages that might follow. I say *might*, because not all people mature into the later stages. In fact, the boundaries of all the stages are fluid. Some young people show great moral wisdom and courage, and some older people seem to be stuck in stage one where "what's right is to get my own way." All of us are capable of reverting to a previous stage for a while, especially when we're stressed or under pressure.

The following is based primarily on the work of Lawrence Kohlberg, Martin Hoffman, John C. Gibbs, and Dr. Lickona. As a reminder: These stages are general guides; a child may enter a stage earlier or later than the model shows.

Stage 0:

1. Newborn reacts to other crying infants by crying
2. Six-month-olds+: comforts *self* when others are distressed

3. <u>One year +</u>: comforts others based on self-interest (you are upsetting me)

Stage 1:

<u>2's and 3's</u>: self-centered morality – "What's right? To get my own way."

<u>4's and 5's</u>: rule-dependent morality – "What's right? To do as I'm told."

Stage 2:

<u>6 – 9</u>: basic equality – "What's right? To be fair to people who are fair to me."

<u>9 – 19</u>: ideal Golden Rule reciprocity – "What's right? To be nice so others will think well of me and I can think well of myself," moving to "What's right? Whatever is good for the group."

Stage 3: Mutual Trust, Intimate Sharing (17-39 years)

According to Gibbs's research, at this point in the maturing process, some people become Type A and some become Type B. Of course, they have been moving toward either A or B during the previous stages, but now they usually settle into one track or the other.

<u>Type A</u>: "My Social Network"

In Stage 3, Type A's make moral judgments according to social consensus.

<u>Type B</u>: Global Network

In Stage 3, Type B's center their moral judgments globally on "what ought to be." They develop a personal moral identity.

Stage 4: The Common Good, Systematized

Type A: "My Social Network"

In Stage 4, the moral decisions of Type A's lean heavily on fixed responsibilities, authorities, and the law.

Type B: Global Network

To Type B's in Stage 4, the ideal is being responsible for contributing to a better society. They hold to the idea of *moral* law and have a personal moral identity.

Postconventional Morality

According to Kohlberg's research, it's uncommon for people to grow into these next three stages, but some do. They exhibit *prosocial behavior*, which means that they act to benefit others without getting any personal reward and possibly at a personal cost.

Stage 5: Principled Perspective

People in Stage 5 believe in social obligation, universal or natural rights, and moral theory, and they act on those beliefs.

Stage 6: Philosophical Perspective (thought-driven)

People in Stage 6 discern and discuss moral issues thoughtfully.

They think in terms of universal principles.

Stage 7: Cosmic Perspective (action-driven)

People in Stage 7 value life from a cosmic, universal standpoint.

They are inspired by a deeper reality in which love is the key.

They are quick to understand and forgive.

They "treasure the spark of humanity in everyone."

They dedicate their lives to humanitarian actions.

They exhibit "the supreme value of self-sacrifice."

Mother Teresa and Gandhi lived in Stage 7, as did Jesus. Most of us will never reach that level, but we may exhibit moral courage from time to time. Like the young man who died shielding his friends from gunfire during the school shooting in Parkland, Florida. Or like volunteers who endangered their own lives to save people during flooding in Houston and elsewhere. That's moral courage. "Greater love has no one than this, that one lay down his life for his friends" (John 15:13).

But in Stage 7, love is for more than just friends: "Love your enemies," said Jesus, "and pray for those who persecute you . . . If you love those who love you, what reward will you get? Are not even the tax collectors doing that? And if you greet only your brothers, what are you doing more than others? Do not even pagans do that? Be perfect, therefore, as your heavenly Father is perfect" (Matthew 5:44-48). That word "perfect" in the original Greek means "whole, undivided, complete, mature." A whole, complete, and mature morality gives itself for all of humanity.

The opposite is what Hoffman refers to as Moral Developmental Delay.[1] That's when someone continues to be

morally immature into adolescence and beyond. A person who is
morally delayed views every issue through a self-centered lens.
Their moral judgment is shallow, and they seem not to
understand reasons for making wise moral choices. In fact, they
often see themselves as victims while seeing their victims as the
offenders.

Does this model of moral development apply only to
Western culture or, more specifically, American society? Or is it
universal? Hoffman says that Kohlberg's stages have been
verified "in over twenty countries or regions around the world."
A friend and mentor of mine, Ken Rideout, confirmed this. He
spent forty years in Thailand as a missionary. Here he tells what
happened one day when he was in China teaching English to
doctors and professors at Beijing Medical University.

.. by 1981, China was beginning to
emerge onto the world stage from the bleakness
and fear of the Cultural Revolution as a new
leader attempted to bring the nation into an era
of openness. Teams of English teachers from
the West had been invite to upgrade education.
So here I was in a hot, colorless city...

I assumed that all my students were
currently Communist, or had been in the past,
for they had spent their lives under atheistic
communism. Religious witnessing had been
forbidden, and Christians had been marked as
ignorant and primitive...

One day, one of the doctors asked, "How do you prove God?"

"You do not prove God," I said. "You *know* God. We prove things in the physical world by experimenting with measurements, weights, chemicals, heat, light, and so on. But you cannot put God in a test tube or measure His dimensions. God is Spirit. Things of the Spirit dimension need no proving, because God's Spirit bears witness to our spirits. God's Spirit confirms the truth of His love and His being."

After some silent thought, the doctors said, "We don't understand."

"Should you lie, rob, murder, or cheat me?" I asked. "Should you take my wife by force? Should you rape my daughter?"

"No!" they answered.

"Are you sure?" I asked.

"Yes," they all said. "We are sure."

"Prove it," I said. "Prove that these things are wrong."

Everyone was silent.

"I agree with you," I said. "We all agree that these things are wrong. I am an American, and you are Chinese. Our language, culture, and political systems are different. Yet on this most important issue for relationship among all people, we agree. There is no need to prove it,

for we all know it. It is a self-evident truth,
universally understood. Things of the Spirit
need no proof, for our Maker has written His
image of love and moral righteousness upon
every human heart. All over the world,
regardless of nation, language, or creed, men
and women, adults and children, educated and
uneducated, all alike know that such behavior is
bad. Each person knows what is good."[2]

God has given each of us the gift of an inner moral
compass. It can become twisted or broken. We can ignore it.
But it's there. And we who are significant adults have the
privilege of helping children learn to use it wisely.

So how do we train our children to grow wise morally?
We know it's not enough to have them memorize the Golden
Rule. Plenty of people can recite the Golden Rule but can't
seem to put it into practice. So how do we help our kids become
morally strong?

Since morality concerns right and wrong, it's easy – and
common – to think that being moral means following rules. But
at its core, morality is not rule-bound. A friend of mine once told
me that she was planning to publish an illustration created by
another friend of mine – but without permission and without
paying. I didn't know if she contractually had the right to use
the art, so I couldn't advise her on the legality of the issue. But I
told her what I did know. "It may be legal," I said, "but it's not
right." Rules are not always right. And what's right is not always
written as a rule.

Acquiescing to conduct imposed by outward rules is one level of morality, and it's necessary in civil society, but it's based on self-interest: I follow the rules

because that will please the one imposing the rule or
because I don't want to get in trouble or
because it permits me to legally get what I want or
because if everyone bucked the rules, we'd have chaos.

The higher forms of morality are not based on rules but on inner drives that govern our moral choices out of respect for others. Moral wisdom comes from a sense of moral identity: This is who I am.

What about the Ten Commandments and all the rules that are in the Old Testament of the Bible? Isn't the Ten Commandments the foundation of our morality?

The children's director at the church I attend explains to children that the Ten Commandments are the ten best ways to live. They tell us how to love God and how to love people. The Ten Commandments are also the cornerstone of God's formation of a functioning government for people who had known only slavery under the despotic rule of the Pharaoh in Egypt. God was training and guiding these people toward maturity, first giving them rules set in stone before guiding them to the mercy and kindness and love shown in Jesus's life and death. The process is not unlike the way we train a child to maturity with our rules "in stone" when they're young and too inexperienced to govern themselves. As children mature and take responsibility for themselves, we set aside the stone, and the rules become a wooden fence and eventually a simple line in the sand. (Although they can be turned back into a fence or even stone if necessary.)

Even with rules carved in stone, God told the Israelites, "I desire mercy not sacrifice" (Hosea 6:6). And the prophet Micah said, "God has showed you, O man, what is good. And what does the Lord require of you? To act justly and to love mercy and to walk humbly with your God" (Micah 6:8).

Jesus quoted Hosea when the religious leaders railed at him for befriending "tax collectors and sinners." He said, "Go and learn what this means: 'I desire mercy, not sacrifice'" (Matthew 9:13). Jesus constantly confronted the teachers of the Law. When one of them asked what the most important commandment was, Jesus answered by quoting the Scripture, "Love the Lord your God with all your heart and with all your soul and with all your mind and with all your strength." Then he added, "The second is this: 'Love your neighbor as yourself.' There is no commandment greater than these" (Mark 12:30, 31).

Rules are paint-by-number. Human/life need is interpretation. Both are valid, and sometimes rules *are* the human/life need of the moment. But it's important to note what rules can and cannot do.

Rules cannot forgive.

Rules cannot have mercy.

Rules do not take circumstances into consideration.

Rules cannot make exceptions.

Rules cannot offer grace.

Because rules are inanimate. Like the law of gravity. If you step off a cliff, gravity doesn't say, "Oops, you took a little misstep there. I won't let you fall this time." No, rules cannot forgive. Forgiveness, mercy, consideration, exceptions, and grace require a human heart, an open heart, an interpretive heart asking, "What does this situation need? What is it that I might not be seeing or hearing? How can I be generous, grateful, and gracious to myself and to others?"

We've done a pretty good job of teaching rules. We've not done as well teaching mercy and the wisdom required to offer it, even though that's what the higher stages of morality are all about. Rules are frozen, but mercy is fluid, which makes it harder to teach. Mercy requires wrestling with our own heart. And yet what does the Lord require of us but to act justly, to love mercy, and to walk humbly with our God?

Part Two:

Practical Ways to Guide Children Toward Moral Wisdom

Chapter 10
Know the Goal

"The only person you are destined to become is the person you decide to be."
– Ralph Waldo Emerson –

So how can we help children internalize good values and morals? First, we have to know what our goal is. That may seem obvious, but we sometimes skip this step. We know we want our kids to "be good" or "be nice." But what do we mean?

Years ago, when I learned to write curricula, I was taught to start each lesson by listing my "behavioral objectives" for the lesson. In other words, I was supposed to note how I wanted children to behave after the lesson, how I hoped it would affect them – specifically, what would they end up knowing, feeling, and doing? So, for example, at the beginning of a lesson plan for four-year-olds on Abraham and the three visitors, I might write: The children will know that Abraham shared his food with three visitors. The children will feel a desire to share. The children will share.

Know, feel, do. I've always found behavioral objectives to be a great way to focus on my goals. Behavioral objectives also serve as a measuring stick to evaluate whether or not I achieved my goal. Was I effective? In reality, I can't see into children's minds to be certain of what they *know*. I can't be sure of what they *feel*. And what they *do* as a result of my lesson may not occur in class but may show up later in the week at home or in school. Still, objectives give me direction and remind me that I'm teaching children, not the material.

So when we teach morality, whether we're parents or classroom teachers, what are our goals? What are we aiming for? Here are my top ten signs of moral wisdom.

1. Responsibility
2. Empathy
3. Self-control
4. Generosity
5. Honesty
6. Gratitude
7. Patience
8. Humility
9. Kindness
10. Love

This is not an exhaustive list, of course, and your top ten might differ from mine. What would you include? What would you exclude? Make your own list. Consider how you would define each virtue on your list, and decide why you think it's an important characteristic of moral wisdom, or as researcher Michele Borba puts it, "moral intelligence." Here are my whys.

1. Responsibility

Responsibility means taking ownership of what we say and do, which is a basic requirement for being a moral person. Responsibility basically means "the ability to respond, to reply." It's based on caring. Being moral means caring about all that

God created – the people, the earth, and the heavens. It means caring about what's happening in the world around us, both in our personal relationships and in society at large. Because we care, we respond by taking *care* of people, the earth, and the heavens. We also take responsibility for how we respond. We can never grow wise morally if we're not willing to take responsibility for our words and actions.

2. Empathy

As I noted previously, according to theorist Martin Hoffman, empathy is *the* goal of moral development. So what is empathy? Like responsibility, empathy is based on caring. Michele Borba defines it as "identifying and feeling other people's concerns."[1] We consider other people's viewpoints. We're *considerate*. We often use a related word: *compassion*, defined as a "sympathetic consciousness of others' distress together with a desire to alleviate it." The apostle Paul was talking about empathy when he said, "Rejoice with those who rejoice; mourn with those who mourn" (Romans 12:15).

3. Self-Control

As Michele Borba puts it, self-control is our "moral muscle." It "helps [a child] use his head to control his emotions" and helps us "put on the brakes." It's often called impulse control. But self-control is not just self-restraint. Self-control works two ways. Not only does it keep us from doing what we believe is wrong, but it also empowers us to do what we believe is right. In that sense, self-control helps us "step on the gas" or "pedal forward" when we need to.

4. Generosity

The act of giving springs from empathy and helps restore the balance of reciprocity that defines morality. Giving in the form of basic sharing is one of the earliest moral lessons we teach children, and we continue to learn the different complexities of sharing as we grow up: sharing with close friends vs. sharing with the homeless, sharing by bank draft vs. sharing in person. As we mature morally, we're more able to be generous in our giving and sharing. Generosity requires us to reach deeper into our pockets and give not out of our abundance but out of what we have good reason to keep for ourselves.

When it comes to generosity, our first thought is probably about giving money. But as essayist Simone Weil pointed out, "Attention is the rarest and purest form of generosity."[2] That's because giving our attention means giving our time, which is often more difficult to give than money.

Generosity is on my list of moral qualities, because morality is based on respect. When we're morally immature, we tend to brush off others, to pass them by, to ignore them and their concerns, to prejudge them, and to treat them as objects or faceless groups. One sign that we're maturing morally is that we become generous with our time and attention toward others. We treat them with dignity, listening to them, considering their concerns, and seeing their individual human worth, the imago dei in each of them.

But there's another reason I include generosity in my top ten: Generosity underpins forgiveness. In fact, *give* is half of the word *forgive*. When we forgive, we give up our demand that someone gets payback for hurting us. We let go of our anger and bitterness toward them. We give up at our attempts to get even. While basic morality operates on the principle of reciprocity, forgiveness does not. It operates on a higher principle: mercy. Forgiveness is an act of generosity. It's generosity of spirit.

5. Honesty

People who are morally wise are honest. They can be trusted. They're clear, open and transparent. They have *integrity*, which in the words of Brené Brown is "choosing to practice your values rather than simply professing them."[3] Integrity means following moral and ethical principles and having high moral character. Integrity integrates our beliefs, values, and experiences into a meaningful whole.

Honest people are also *ethical*, which means, by definition, that they adhere to "high standards of honest and honorable dealing, . . . especially in the professions or in business." Some of Jesus's strongest rebukes were directed toward corrupt, dishonest, unethical religious leaders. "You belong to your father, the devil," he said, "and you want to carry out your father's desires. He was a murderer from the beginning, not holding to the truth, for there is no truth in him. When he lies, he speaks his native language, for he is a liar and the father of lies" (John 8:44). This straight talk from Jesus was meant to shake up and wake up those who were supposed to be leading people to truth.

Honesty honors the imago dei within us. In our dealings with other people, honesty shows that we're morally strong. There can be no morality without honesty.

6. <u>Gratitude</u>

One of the first moral lessons we teach children is how to respect people by using good manners. And one of our first lessons in manners is how to say, "Please" and "Thank you." Gratitude, expressed as manners is important, but it's only a start. Mature gratitude is heart-felt and overflows in actions that give back or pass it on. In that sense, gratitude is linked with generosity.

Diana Butler Bass recently wrote an entire book on gratitude entitled *Grateful: The Transformative Power of Giving Thanks*. She links heart-felt gratitude to moral action: "[Y]ou might define gratitude as social responsibility that demands action through public commitments to charity, stewardship, volunteerism, and social institutions. You believe that gratitude is an essential foundation of civic life."[4]

I like to think of gratitude as *appreciation*, because that seems to deepen its meaning. Appreciation recognizes the value of something - or someone - and acknowledges their worth and quality. In fact, appreciation *increases* the value of whatever or whoever is appreciated. Which gets back to respect - morality. As we grow more mature morally, we increasingly value the worth and quality of others. Our gratitude deepens, along with our reverence, wonder, and awe for all that God created.

7. <u>Patience</u>

The most impatient people in the world are infants. They have no problem letting us know that they want something, although what that something is, we don't always know. But they make it clear that they want it *now*. They are demanding, but we understand that they are not yet making a conscious moral choice. Fast forward to adulthood, and that same demanding behavior is a sure sign of moral immaturity. People of high moral character have learned patience, a quality that is essential for relating to other people.

Patience, in psychological terms, can be called "deferred gratification," the ability to wait to get something we really want or to wait to be rewarded for spending time and effort to achieve a goal. When we have to be patient over a long period of time, we call it perseverance or endurance.

Patience is also what allows us to be "slow to anger," another essential for respecting others. "Everyone should be quick to listen, slow to speak and slow to become angry," wrote James, "for man's anger does not bring about the righteous life that God desires" (James 1:19-20, NIV).

For young children, I define patience as waiting without complaining. When children are able to wait without complaining and to defer gratification, that tells us they're growing toward moral maturity.

8. Humility

A comic strip taught me a life-changing lesson about humility:

Snoopy sits at his typewriter on the roof of his doghouse, telling Charlie Brown that he's writing a book on theology. Charlie Brown says he hopes Snoopy has a good title. Snoopy says he does: "Have You Ever Considered That You Might Be Wrong?"[5]

When I read that, I realized for the first time that I had never considered that I might be wrong. How arrogant of me! I had been thinking I was right about all the important things. But I'm not. I'm wrong about many things. You are too. It's just that we don't know what those things are – until we do. The more I know, the more I realize how much I don't know.

Humility is acknowledging that there is a great deal that we do not know. There's always someone who knows more than we do. Humility also acknowledges that whatever we do, we are not the best. There's always someone who will do it better. And humility is fine with that.

According to ancient Jewish philosopher Bahya ibn Paquda, "All virtues and duties are dependent on humility." Taking responsibility? Yes. Empathy? Yes. Self-control, generosity, honesty? Yes. Gratitude? Definitely. Moral wisdom can't exist without humility.

Being humble includes repenting, which means being able to say, "I'm sorry" and trying to turn a hurtful situation around, making amends as best we can.

Being humble also includes tolerance. That may sound strange – morality can't tolerate immorality, right? Right. But that's not what I'm talking about. Michele Borba explains it well in *Building Moral Intelligence*: "Tolerance does not require that we suspend moral judgment . . . it does require that we respect *differences*." Madeleine Albright, a former U.S. Secretary of State, who has worked with many people of different beliefs, races, and cultures, says she doesn't like to use the term *tolerance*, because it has the connotation of "putting up with" someone or something. Instead, she prefers to use the term *respect*.[6] That's really what tolerance is. All people are created in God's image. All deserve to be treated with love and respect, even if we disagree with their beliefs or behavior.

The apostle Paul said, "I try to find common ground with everyone" (1 Corinthians 9:22). Humility says both, "What can I bring to the table?" and "What can I learn at the table?".

9. Kindness

Eleanor Roosevelt, in the introduction to the *Book of Common Sense Etiquette*, wrote, "The basis of all good human behavior is kindness."[7] Kindness is a broad umbrella that can encompass a wide range of behaviors. In Old English, *kind* (spelled cynd) meant family or lineage. Generally, people favor their family (or in olden days, their tribe), treating them with more kindness and grace than they give to people outside the family. So kindness is treating someone with grace and favor.

When Jesus was asked what the greatest commandment was, he said, "'Love the Lord your God with all your heart and with all your soul and with all your strength and with all your mind' and 'Love your neighbor as yourself'" (Luke 10:27). Father Thomas Hopko suggests that this last part means, "Love your neighbors as if they were one of you," meaning one of your family, one of your group, one of your own "tribe."[8] That means treating others with the same kindness, favor, and grace that we would grant to people in our own families and social groups.

When I think of people who have been kind to me, the person at the top of the list is a writing mentor who believed in me and encouraged me. She took the time to get to know me, and when I was with her, I had her full attention. She made me feel important and welcome in her world. What's more, she treated everyone this way. Encouraging the good in others, being considerate, gracious, and helpful – that's what it is to be kind.

"Feel how when you extend a kindness, however simple, you are energized and not depleted," says Krista Tippett in her book *Becoming Wise*. "Scientists, again, are proving that acts of kindness and generosity are literally infectious, passing from stranger to stranger to stranger. Kindness is an everyday byproduct of all the great virtues, love most especially."[9]

10. Love

All ten of the moral qualities in my list overlap. As with Russian stacking dolls, one opens to reveal another inside, which opens to reveal yet another. Inside responsibility is empathy, and inside empathy is self-control, and inside self-control is kindness, and so on and so on until at the core, we find Love. Not because love is the smallest but because it's the force that energizes all the others and holds them together. "The greatest of these is love" (1 Corinthians 13).

What, then, is love?

The answer is not so much *what* as *who*. "God is love" (1 John 4:16). Love is the Creator and Source of life. Jesus is Love in the flesh, Love incarnate, Love in person. The Holy Spirit animates imago dei in us. And because we're created in the image of God, we recognize love in Jesus. We see love in the way he treated people, in what he did and how he spoke.

Because of imago dei, we are primed to sense when we're being loved and when we're not. We know that if someone loves us, they will respect and trust us. They will treat us with kindness, dignity, honor, consideration, generosity, grace, and mercy – at least most of the time. Of course, the converse is true as well: If we love someone, we will respect and trust them. We will treat them with kindness, dignity, honor, consideration, generosity, grace, and mercy – at least most of the time. None of us is perfect. We all have our crabby days. Sometimes we're inconsiderate toward the people we love. Sometimes we discourage them. Sometimes they're inconsiderate and discourage us. But real love returns to respect, honor, and kindness as the norm of the relationship. The modus operandi. The foundation.

In the 1800s, writer Dinah Mulock Craik, in her book *A Life for a Life*, wrote, "Oh, the comfort – the inexpressible comfort of feeling *safe* with a person – having neither to weigh thoughts, nor measure words, but pouring them all right out, just as they are, chaff and grain together; certain that a faithful hand will take and sift them, keep what is worth keeping, and then with the breath of kindness blow the rest away." That's love.

Becca Stevens, founder of Thistle Farms, a business set up to "heal, empower, and employ women survivors of trafficking, prostitution, and addiction," recently wrote a book entitled *Love Heals*.[10] In an Instagram post on Easter weekend, 2018, she wrote, "Let this be a day of the simple power of love as a force for change. Let love be your mantra today. Love, love, love. Let love inform our work, our interactions, our rituals, our marketing, our parenting, our economies, our politics. Keeping it simple helps love's power be realized. Love, love, love." Part of the Thistle Farms mission statement says, "We believe that in the end, love is the most powerful force for change in the world."

Responsibility, empathy, self-control, generosity, honesty, gratitude, patience, humility, kindness, and love. Those are my ten essential signs of a fully functioning moral compass. As you may have noticed, several of them are known as fruits of the Spirit: "love, joy, peace, patience, kindness, goodness, faithfulness, gentleness, and self-control" (Galatians 5:22, 23).

That brings me to one more important point before we move into practical ways to guide our children into moral wisdom: "In [God] we live and move and have our being" (Acts 17:28). The reverse is true as well: In us God lives and moves and has being. Imago dei. The point? We are not alone in our efforts to grow morally wise. We have the help of God's Spirit.

Chapter 11
Speak to be Echoed, Act to be Copied

"[B]ehavior is generally learned
by imitating observed experiences,
so the more examples of caring our kids witness,
the greater the chance
that those will be the behaviors they copy."
– Michele Borba, *Building Moral Intelligence* –

As my sixteen-year-old son and I stepped out of the Department of Motor Vehicles, I tossed him the keys to my car. He had just earned his driver's license. I swallowed my nervous mom worries and said, "You drive us home." I knew that was what my dad would have done for me. He always treated me with a generous grace that told me he trusted me and believed in me. Now here I was, able to grant the same to my son. But now I could see from the parent's perspective. As my son drove home, and I worked at keeping my backseat driver's mouth shut, I realized that my own driving habits had been his example.

Now I'm a pretty good driver. I've never gotten a ticket. But in that moment, I realized that perhaps nothing confronts us with the power of our own modeling like handing the keys of our car to our newly licensed teen. All of a sudden, it matters a great deal if we often exceeded the speed limit, if we swore at another driver, if we texted that time when we knew we shouldn't have. Our children were watching. We know they may make some bad choices, but it's awful to think, *what if they make those bad choices because they first saw us make them?*

Adulthood carries a strong allure for children. After all, adults get to decide how late to stay up. They get to decide what to eat and when. They get to watch shows that kids aren't allowed to watch. They get to drive and go interesting places. Adults decide how to spend their time and money. It's a privilege to be an adult.

At least that's what it often looks like to children. They want to act grown up, so they watch us to see how a grown-up acts. What does a grown-up do when they're angry? Sad? Frustrated? Worried? Happy? Children learn what adults do by watching and listening to adults.

The following chapters suggest practical ways to teach morality. But all of those tools are based on the premise that we adults are 1) communicating our expectations about what's right and wrong and 2) modeling those expectations ourselves. Modeling, says Michele Borba, is "one of the oldest and simplest psychology premises: 'The more you see it, the more likely you'll become it.'"

We can teach all the lessons in the world, we can preach until we lose our voices, and we can construct a million activities to teach morality, but if we're not living what we teach, all those lessons will lose their meaning. That's one reason children leave church when they get old enough to make that decision for themselves. "Our best and brightest are leaving," moaned one children's director. Of course, they are. Our best and brightest find the exit first, but lots of others find their way out as well, because they're not blind or deaf, and they're certainly not stupid. When the way we act doesn't match what we've taught, they respond the way Jesus did: "You hypocrites!"

So the first issues to look at are personal to us. Who and what do we criticize? How? Who and what do we admire and praise? How? Who and what do we find funny? How do we speak about sermons after church? Who and what do we support verbally or with our time and money? What do we choose to turn a blind eye to? It matters, because we are constantly showing children how adults act.

I'm not saying that we have to be perfect. We won't be, even if we try, and it's best not to pretend that we are. Kids need us to do the best we can. When we mess up, they need us to admit it, to try to make things right, and to get back up and try again. That's part of modeling what a good, moral person does.

The first principle, then, of guiding children toward moral wisdom is one that only we can give: Speak to be echoed and act to be copied.

"Act as if people are watching you,
because they are.
The trail you leave behind starts now."
– Seth Godin –

Chapter 12
Respect Children

"Children will not learn to accept and tolerate
differences in others
if they have not experienced acceptance and tolerance
for their differences."
– Clyde W. Ford, *We Can All Get Along* –

If you're a trained teacher or enjoy being around children, then you probably already respect them. But plenty of people become parents or volunteer Sunday school teachers without recognizing the importance of respecting children in the same way we respect adults. Respect for children requires being considerate of them. We *consider* their situation and point of view. We're thoughtful about them. We don't dismiss them but take them seriously. We validate them as worthy human beings, as *imago dei.*

Respecting children means that we do all we can to make sure they feel welcome and safe in our presence. That's easier to do when we enjoy being with a child. Some children are hard to enjoy, just as some adults are hard to enjoy. We respect them anyway. So specifically, what does respecting children look like?

• Pay attention to children. Notice what's new with them (haircut, shoes, jacket . . .). See them, and let them know that you see.

• Listen to children. If possible, physically get on their level to communicate – as one educator put it, "Eye to eye and heart to heart." We'll take a closer look at communication later.

• Let children teach you something. There's a good chance that children know something valuable that you don't know, whether it's counting in a foreign language or coding skills. It's a valuable practice to turn the tables and let them be the knowledgeable people once in a while.

• Speak respectfully to children. Don't condescend or talk down to them.

• Get to know children as individuals. If you're a parent, you have the privilege of witnessing the emergence of a person who is unique in all the world. If you're a teacher, you have the privilege of spending a few weeks or months getting to know these unique young people. Try not to let a previous teacher's opinion color your attitude toward a child. In fact, if someone is gossiping about a child (this goes for adults as well), politely bow out of the conversation. And be discerning. Disparaging information about a child or family sometimes comes disguised as a prayer need.

• Make allowances for the child's age and level of understanding, but also allow for individual differences in children's growth. It's tempting to compare children, measuring the growth of one against the growth of another, but that's not really fair to children or to yourself. Listen and watch to see where each child is coming from and what they understand.

"We love because (God) first loved us" (1 John 4:19). The apostle John may not have known it, but he was setting out one of the most important principles of helping our children become morally wise: passing it on. We tend to pass on what was passed to us. We love others because someone first loved us.

This principle is not limited to love. We are honest with others because someone was first honest with us. We encourage others because someone first encouraged us. We respect others because we were first respected. This is basic. If we want our children to respect others (including us), then we must first respect them. We must treat them with courtesy and grace.

Chapter 13
Have Rules and Communicate Them

"If a thing is right, it *can* be done,
and if it is wrong, it *can be done without*;
and a good man will find a way."
– Anna Sewell, *Black Beauty* –

Most new parents have never taken child development courses, and many have never spent much time with children. Sunday school teachers are often volunteers who get little training if any. They go into the classroom focused on the material and start teaching, only to get frustrated when some of the children behave as if they don't have a clue as to how to act in a classroom. They assume that children should automatically know how to behave. But they don't. Not unless the teacher has set some ground rules.

A few years ago, I was talking with another teacher about how I let kids choose the way they want to sit when they gather as a large group. Because I've studied learning styles, I know that different people learn best in different physical positions. So I let my kids sit in a chair, or on the floor cross-legged, or sprawled on their stomachs. It doesn't matter to me as long as they are paying attention and not bothering other kids. But the teacher I was speaking with was appalled. To maintain discipline in her classroom, she insists that all children sit straight in their chairs, feet on the floor. Who is right?

There's actually no right or wrong when it comes to the way to sit. My friend was stricter, I was more lenient. The key to running a class smoothly is to clearly communicate the rules and be consistent. Thinking our way is the only way – or the only *right* way – is simply not true, and comparing ourselves to other teachers is a distraction.

The same holds true at home. Comparing ourselves to other parents is unproductive. Thinking that our method of childrearing is the only way – or the only *right* way – is simply not true. Again, the key is being as clear and consistent as possible. And if you see that the rules you've set don't fit your children's needs, be willing to flex and change the rules.

At home or in the classroom, let children know what you expect of them in different situations. If your rules are general enough at the outset – for example, speak kindly, keep our house/classroom neat – then the details of each can be worked out as needed.

Here are some specifics to consider as you set and communicate rules:

• State rules in the positive if possible. Tell children what you want instead of what you don't want. That helps them understand exactly what you expect. For example, say, "Walk quietly" instead of, "Don't run," because "don't run" leaves other options open. Children can skip, twirl, or tumble, and they're still following the rule.

• Let children help make the rules. Tell them the issue that needs to be addressed, like rude talk or hoarding the crayons, and ask them what rules they would suggest.

• Post the rules on the wall as a reminder if you need to, especially for younger children. For those who can't read, draw a picture symbolizing the rule. Stick with just the few most important rules.

• Know that you'll have to remind kids about what the rule is. It can be exasperating to have to repeat rules for the umpteenth time, but a calm, firm reminder is more effective than losing your temper. (And it models self- control.)

• Consistently enforce the rules with a good dose of grace and mercy. How? We'll look more closely at behavior management in a later chapter.

Chapter 14
Give Kids an Emotion Vocabulary

"It's not easy to learn to whistle
if there's no one to show you how."
– Janusz Korczak, *King Matt the First* –

Remember that important milestone in moral development called perspective-taking? It enables us to see from another person's point of view, to understand that they are afraid or frustrated or overjoyed or worried. Perspective-taking is possible because all humans feel the same emotions no matter how different we may be in culture, nationality, race, gender, or age. So paying attention to how people feel and labeling those emotions gives kids an emotional vocabulary. "He's frustrated right now." "She looks really hopeful." "I think he's worried." "Do you think she might be afraid?" This helps children develop empathy.

Teaching children to recognize their own emotions is important as well. For younger children, it's as simple as, "You're angry, aren't you?" Or "You're so eager you can hardly wait." With older kids, we can fit our comments into the course of conversation. "You look surprised. What were you expecting?" Or "You seem disappointed. So what will you do now?" Then it's good to pause and give the child time to confirm our assessment or to correct us. If we say, "You look scared," the child may answer, "No, I'm just worried." Recognizing our own emotions and talking about the way we feel helps us handle our feelings in wise and healthy ways. It's a step toward self-control.

For older children, we might refer to a current event. It could be local to their school or neighborhood, or it could be national or international. We might say something like, "Wow! I can only begin to imagine how that person must feel. What about you?" We can also do this with historical events or fictional stories told in movies, books, and television. We can even ask these questions about Bible stories.

Perspective-taking and identifying emotions is a stepping stone toward rejoicing with those who rejoice, mourning with those who mourn, and actually helping others if and when it's appropriate. First empathy and then, "How can I help?"

Chapter 15
Teach the Importance of Small Acts

"Sow a thought and you reap an act;
sow an act and you reap a habit;
sow a habit and you reap a character;
sow a character and you reap a destiny."
– Charles Reade –

In his book *The Road to Character*, David Brooks wrote, "You become more disciplined, considerate, and loving through a thousand small acts of self-control, sharing, service, friendship, and refined enjoyment. If you make disciplined, caring choices, you are slowly engraving certain tendencies into your mind. You are making it more likely that you will desire the right things and execute the right actions."[1]

Small acts seem doable. One small act leads to two. Two can become ten. Ten can become one hundred, five hundred, a thousand. "A thousand small acts."

As I write this, one of the big stories in the news is the safe landing of a Southwest jet after its engine exploded in flight.[2] News reporters speak in awe of the pilot's calm as she talked to air traffic controllers and piloted her jet to safety. That calm and skill did not happen overnight. Tammie Jo Shults had trained and flown for years, making a thousand small decisions that gave her the mental, emotional, and physical muscle to bring her plane down safely and save hundreds of lives.

The mental, emotional, spiritual, and sometimes physical muscle needed to make major moral choices – and make them wisely – rarely just appears the moment we need it. That strength develops through exercising our moral muscle many times a day through a thousand small acts.

• Teach and model good manners at home and in the classroom, starting with "please" and "thank you." Very young children can learn "please" and "thank you" in sign language even before they can talk.

• Teach and model the small tasks that make your home or classroom run smoothly, with everyone pitching in – picking up, cleaning, organizing.

• Teach kids how to compromise, advises Michele Borba. "You give up a little, the other person gives up a little." Model compromising. When you compromise with children, point it out: "Let's compromise. I'll give a little on this, and you give a little."

• Help kids figure out ways to get back in control when they lose it. And model ways that work for you when *you're* about to lose it. Michele Borba suggests taking a walk, listening to soothing music, thinking of a peaceful place, deep breathing, stretching, or shooting baskets. When one of my grandsons was struggling with anger, I guided him through a process I call,

"Half It." HALF is an acronym for Hands, Abdomen, Lungs, Face. When we're tense with worry, anger, or stress, our hands often curl into fists. Our abdomen often tightens or feels jittery. Our breathing becomes shallow. Our face feels it too: clenched jaws, a scowl, narrowed eyes. So take that tension and HALF it:

Hands, relax. (Shake them if you need to.)

Abdomen relax. (Soften your belly.)

Lungs relax. (Breathe deeply through your nose. Exhale slowly through your mouth.)

Face relax. (Unclench your teeth and jaw. Raise your eyebrows. Blink and refocus.)

Still tense? HALF it again. And again. And again if necessary.

Even young children can do this, although if they're too young to spell, the acronym won't mean anything. You can coach them, "Hands, belly, breath, face."

• Ask, "Who can we help today?" I was assisting in our local botanical garden's "Tuesday for Tots" program on the day that they were making construction paper trees to celebrate the Jewish day of Tu B'Shevat. One four-year-old asked for a second piece of paper. "I want to make one for my sister," he said. "She couldn't come today." It was a small gift, but a very important one. As you go through your day with children, periodically challenge them with, "Who could we give one to? Who could we make one for? Who can we honor today? Who can we cheer up today? How?"

Sometimes small acts have big results. Bend life toward goodness. Bend each day toward goodness. Bend each hour toward goodness.

Chapter 16
Give Specific Feedback

"The object of teaching a child
is to enable him to get along without his teacher."
– Elbert Hubbard –

When I was taking classes for a Master's Degree in writing, I was mentored each semester by a different award-winning author. Each one coached me on my writing and critiqued my manuscripts. One semester, my mentor was Susan Fletcher. The first time Susan returned one of my manuscripts, I was surprised to see that she had not only marked the places that needed work, but she had also marked the places she liked, the lines she thought I had gotten right. She even drew little hearts beside paragraphs that she loved. I hadn't realized until that moment how helpful it was to be told exactly what I was doing right. Once I could see what I did right, I not only knew what target to aim for, but I also knew I could hit it.

When we give children specific feedback, focusing primarily on what they do right, it helps direct them toward doing it again. Of course, sometimes we also have to point out what they do wrong. In either case, it's best to avoid generic dog-training language ("Good boy!" "Bad girl!"). Instead, label the *act* specifically.

- "Thank you for sharing. That was *generous* of you."

- "You picked up the towel I dropped. That was very *thoughtful.*"
- "You spoke up for the new girl. That took *courage.*"
- "You let him go first. That was very *courteous.*"

If you're a teacher, try to compliment children in front of their parents once in a while. "Gracie is one of the most considerate kids I know." "Daniel asks the most interesting questions. He's a deep thinker."

A warning: When you address a misbehavior, take care. Make sure you label the behavior, not the child. For example, instead of saying, "You're so rude," say "That was a rude tone of voice." Also, make sure that you've read the situation correctly and are not falsely accusing a child. My mother once told me, "You're just an ingrate." In reality, I was upset, because I had been too shy and scared to speak out. I was also too shy to correct her. You can see, too, that she addressed my character and not my behavior. I don't say this to demean my mother. She was a good, godly woman. My point is that accusing a child wrongly can cut deep, especially if the comment is directed to the child's character as opposed to the behavior.

It's important for children to see themselves as moral. As we saw earlier, one of the signs that children are maturing morally is that they think of themselves as being morally wise. In other words, in their own minds, being moral is part of their identity: "That's who I am." We can help them find and use their moral compass by mirroring back to them a positive moral vision of themselves.

Chapter 17
Teach the Whys

"I kept six honest serving-men
(They taught me all I know);
Their names are What and Why and When
And How and Where and Who."
– Rudyard Kipling –

As we teach morals, it's best to tell children reasons for why the behavior or attitude is a poor moral choice or a wise one. When I was growing up, the "why" often came down to, "Because I'm the parent (or teacher) and I said so." That sets up the parent or teacher as the reason to behave, which means that whenever the parent or teacher is not present, the child has no internal reason to make the wise moral choice. Daniel J. Siegel, writing about the teen brain, said, "Choosing not to get a tattoo at an unknown place because you value your health is very different from saying 'I won't do it because my mother told me not to.'"[1] Do children a favor and give them concrete reasons to make wise choices.

On the other hand, avoid going into long lectures about why something is right or wrong. That's what I tend to do, presenting all the reasons I can think of. I say, "In the first place . . . and in the second place . . ." One day when my younger son was about seven, and I had refused to allow him to do something (I don't even remember now what it was), he looked up at me and asked, "What's the first place?" He was bracing himself for the lecture. The thing is, lectures are not very effective. Children remember the first thing we say and the last thing. The information in between gets lost. It's best to keep explanations short and simple.

One of the best reasons for making a wise choice is safety or health. In classrooms, I've often told children, "My job is to keep you safe and healthy, so I can't allow you to do that, because it might hurt someone." Or we can give a reason that focuses on the way life works best. We do that naturally in all sorts of situations from the time children are small. "Don't touch the stove," we say. Why? It's often hot, and you might get burned. "Cover your mouth when you sneeze." Why? So you won't spread germs and make someone sick. "Don't leave your toy trucks on the stairs." Why? Because someone might trip over them and fall - and that someone might be you. On the surface, these may not seem like moral situations, but morality is operative when we are *careful*, caring whether others get sick or hurt. In addition, pointing out cause and effect in non-moral situations - like touching a hot stove - lays the groundwork for understanding the cause and effect principle of morality. Why should we make the wise moral choice? Because it's the way life works best.

I find it helpful to look at Bible teachings the same way: less as "rules" and more as "this is the way life works best." When we look at Jesus's teachings from this viewpoint, we see that the "whys" are built in.

• "Blessed are the merciful . . ." Why? ". . . for they will be shown mercy" (Matthew 5:7). This is not a rule; it's just the way life usually works. If you're a merciful person, others tend to treat you with mercy as well. It's reciprocity at work. An eye for an eye.

• "Do not judge, or you too will be judged. For in the same way you judge others, you will be judged" (Matthew 7:1, 2). This is not a rule and a corresponding threat of God's punishment. It's simply the way life usually works. If we judge others, they will judge us as well. Even if they don't judge us, we *think* they are judging us (because we ourselves are judgmental). What's more, we secretly judge ourselves in the same measure.

• "Forgive, and you will be forgiven. Give, and it will be given to you . . . For with the measure you use, it will be measured to you" (Luke 6:37, 38). This has less to do with God forgiving us than with the damage we do to ourselves when we don't forgive. To the degree that we hold onto bitterness and resentment, we hold onto what hurt us in the first place. In other words, it's impossible to be free of the wound, because we're clinging to it. We're released as much as we release others. That's not a divine mandate; it's simply the way life works. Wishing someone else ill does nothing to make us feel whole. Forgiving is healthy.

The basic "why" of morality is as simple as "you reap what you plant" (Galatians 6:7).

Chapter 18
Challenge Kids to Think

"If I look confused it's because I'm thinking."
- Samuel Goldwyn -

Discerning right from wrong requires thought. The moral thought process grows from "Will I be rewarded for this or punished?" to "What will they think of me if I do (or don't do) this?" to "This is who I am and what I stand for." Through his research on morality, Kohlberg came to the conclusion that we can nudge children to think beyond the stage they are in – but only one stage beyond. Still, that's a worthwhile goal.

So how do we nudge children to think?

• Talk with children about morality.

Discuss what morality is. Ask how we can tell when someone has good moral values. Avoid lecturing. Instead, include the child's viewpoint by asking open-ended questions. Michele Borba suggests asking, "What is a conscience?" Ask challenging questions like, "What's the difference between cheating and helping a friend with his lessons?" Also give kids a chance to come up with challenging questions for you to wrestle with.

• Teach TOP.

That's an acronym suggested by researcher and professor John C. Gibbs.[1] I've used it with my own grandchildren. In fact, I posted TOP on an index card on my refrigerator as a reminder. It means "Think of the Other Person," and it comes with a "secret code" – patting the top of your head. Anytime we catch ourselves or our kids treating others in a care-less way, we can remind them, "Think of the other person" or simply pat the top of our head.

• Practice "finding the good."

When someone (child or adult) criticizes or complains about another person, then challenge them to say something positive about that person or something about that person to be grateful for.

• Use deep-thought questions.

For older kids, deep-thought questions/statements can become points of discussion. The following are from Timothy Keller's book *The Reason for God*:[2]

"There is no absolute truth." (Is that an absolute truth?)

"You shouldn't believe something you can't prove." (Prove it.)

"Is morality relative?" (Are there things that most people, regardless of their personal beliefs, think others should stop doing? Genocide? Child abuse? etc.)

• Use deep-thought conversation starters.

Here's an example that comes from Katherine Boo's book *Behind the Beautiful Forevers*:

"Wealthy citizens accused the slum-dwellers (in Mumbai, India) of making the city filthy and unliveable, even as an oversupply of human capital kept the wages of their maids and chauffeurs low."[3] Exploring that statement can keep a conversation going for a while.

We can find plenty more conversation starters in the daily news. And we should be prepared for kids to see straight to the heart of the situation. They'll usually speak their minds if we're willing to close our mouths and listen.

Chapter 19
Provide Social Interaction

"Compassion grows with the inner recognition
that your neighbour shares your humanity with you.
This partnership cuts through all walls
which might have kept you separate."
- Henri J.M. Nouwen -

Perspective-taking, which is crucial to maturing morally, develops through interacting with peers, participating in groups, taking on different roles in school and other communities, and interacting with parents and other significant adults. There's a unique kind of joy that comes from opening our hands and hearts to others.

In these days of being wary and staying safe, we often operate in fear mode, pulling back from people and keeping our children in a protective bubble. We often perceive other beliefs and worldviews as threatening instead of enlightening. So while we're willing to give our kids social experiences, we may limit those experiences to interactions with people who share our own beliefs or economic status.

Besides, if we venture beyond our own social borders, our kids might hear bad language. We may have to shake hands with someone who's not clean or interrupt our schedule to deal with someone who we think should have been more responsible.

But Jesus is already there. Maybe we should be there too. Maybe we need to develop a level of tolerance for being outside our comfort zone. So . . .

• Involve kids in community-helping activities.

Provide food and clothing for the poor. When disaster relief is needed, find a way to contribute money, goods, or a helping hand. Help elderly neighbors. Find ways to extend a welcome to immigrants and people who are lonely or new to the community.

• Have a "secret kindness pal."

Draw names or choose a person to do anonymous acts of kindness for.

• Host a family visiting from another country.

Through one of our local colleges, my son and his family signed up to host a Pakistani family that was in the U.S. so their mother could earn an advanced degree in education. My son's family often had the Pakistani family over for meals or other events, and the Pakistani family had us all over for a traditional Pakistani meal.

• Learn to say one word in several different languages.

"Peace" or "hello" or "love" or "welcome" are easy to learn in a variety of languages. You could also learn gestures that are customary greetings, like the slight head-bow of the Japanese.

• Join groups that include members of a variety of backgrounds.

Sports teams, art classes, play groups, scouts – choose groups that are inclusive of all types of people and not comprised solely of kids from your own demographic.

• Extend hospitality to a variety of people.

Invite people to dinner who are older or of a different race or nationality or background. If they reciprocate, let them host you. Ask them to tell their stories. Then listen. Accept and even enjoy your differences, emphasizing what you have in common. Michele Borba points out that intolerance and stereotyping often result from simply not knowing people who are different from us – elderly people; people of different races, religions, and nationalities; people with disabilities. Dr. Thomas Lickona suggests that we "learn what is interesting, useful, and enriching about other ways of thinking and living and benefit from such exposure."[1]

• Help each other avoid stereotyping.

In *Teaching Tolerance*, Sara Bullard suggests that families or classes agree to say "check that" when sweeping statements are made[2] – by them, by you, in news reports, on TV, in movies, or on social media – statements like, "They always . . .," "They never . . .," "All of them are . . .," "Cheerleaders (or other groups) are all . . ." Talk about why we might say that, why those are false statements, and why they are harmful. Help each other discover similarities between people of different races, religions, nationalities, and beliefs. Get into the habit of looking at others with interest and thoughtfulness. Ask what we can learn from them. What do they bring to the table?

> "Life's most persistent and urgent question is,
> 'What are you doing for others?'"
> – Martin Luther King –

Chapter 20
Link Teaching Activities to Moral Choices

"Everything's got a moral if only you can find it."
– Lewis Carroll, *Alice's Adventures in Wonderland* –

My dad says, "Wise people learn from experience, and wiser people learn from someone else's experience." As you go through your day, point out moral cause-and-effect to your children, not in a lecturing way but simply by casually remarking on it. "Wow! Did you see that? He went out of his way to help that older man." Or "Ouch! I'd feel awful if someone spoke to me the way that woman spoke to the waiter." If you begin this when children are young, it won't be long until they are pointing out moral cause-and-effect to you.

If you're a teacher, be alert for moral situations in lessons and activities in your classroom. The following is a brief list of activities geared toward moral development. Some are more suited to the classroom, but they can be adapted for use at home. (And just so you know, I am not affiliated or getting paid by any of the sites or sources I mention here.)

- "Who Am I?"
  Have kids write an anonymous description of themselves. (Tell them that you'll be reading these descriptions aloud. That way, they won't divulge something they'd rather

keep private.) Shuffle the self-descriptions and read them aloud. After each one, ask the class to guess who wrote it. This encourages children to think about each other and really see each other. For older kids, discuss the difference between how we see ourselves and how we think others see us. Talk about character vs. image: What is character? What is image? How do they show up each day? Is one more important than the other? If so, which one and why?

- Books and movies

Ask kids to compare themselves to a book's characters. Ask: Who do you identify with and why? What would you have done in the same situation? Is there a clear right and wrong choice, or did the character(s) have two choices that both seemed to be right (or wrong)? Tell about a time when you had to decide between two choices that both seemed right. (You can find a limited list of classic children's books and movies categorized by the value each exemplifies at teachingvalues.com. I have no connection with this site but think the list provides a good service, although I wish it were more extensive.)

- Art

Have students draw "graphic novel" type illustrations for a hero story of their choice. Graphic novels are books in comic-book format. Discuss why kids (or the world at large) consider the main character (or another character) to be a hero.

- History

History is about people's choices and the consequences that resulted. The magazine *Cobblestone* is a good source for stories about American History for kids nine to fourteen. The articles make good discussion starters. Talk about historical decisions that were moral. What made the decision a moral one? It's easy to look back and see that a particular decision was wrong (or right), but could the person who made the choice have known how it would turn out? How do we know what choices to make in our time?

• Science, Math, Geography, the Arts

All these involve people, their stories, and their choices. Ask kids to select a scientist, mathematician, explorer, or artist whose story inspires them and write the best part of that person's life on a "story card" (a large index card). *Faces* magazine, for kids age nine to fourteen, contains articles about people around the world and provides a good way for kids to grow in understanding and empathy. Another source, appropriate for teens, is David Brooks's book *The Road to Character.* Each chapter tells real life stories that illustrate the growth of character. Brooks says, "[M]oral improvement occurs most reliably when the heart is warmed, when we come into contact with people we admire and love and we consciously and unconsciously bend our lives to mimic theirs."¹ That's the benefit of studying the challenges and choices of a person we admire.

• Coat of Arms

Ask children to draw a shield on a piece of copy paper. (A large U with a line across the top works.) Then they draw a vertical line down the center of the shield and a horizontal line across the middle. In each of these four sections, they draw a symbol of something they value highly. Discuss how knights sometimes carried shields marked with the symbol of the family or king they worked for. They would carry standards – flags or banners marked with those symbols – into battle. Ask: What values are you willing to stand up for? What are people today willing to fight and die for?

• Wise Sayings

Post wise, inspirational quotes on the wall, and leave them up for a while. One that I posted on a mirror in our hallway was, "The most important thing you wear is your smile." Discuss the quotes if your kids are open to it. Otherwise, simply leave the quotes on the wall as a subtle bit of inspiration to be read by whoever needs it – including you. Challenge your kids to post quotes that they find inspiring. They could even make a book of collected quotes and illustrate it themselves, adding sayings as they come across them.

• Current Events

Be on the lookout for morally relevant events that occur in your family or neighborhood, in your city or state, in your nation or the world and discuss them, suggests Michele Borba in *Building Moral Intelligence.* She gives the example of one mother who used the advice column "Dear Abby" to read and discuss with her family.

Part Three:

Challenges

Chapter 21
More About Communication

"There is only one rule for being a good talker -
learn to listen."
- Christopher Morley -

On Saturday of the weekend after 9/11, I was scheduled to speak to a group of teachers about the stages of child development. As I drove to the conference, the skies were silent, empty of planes, and I, like everyone else, was in shock. I was also deep in thought, reconsidering my presentation. There was no way I could present my usual sessions. We would need to address what had happened. What's more, these teachers would be going into their Sunday school classrooms the day after my presentation. Somehow, they would need to talk with children, on the children's level, about what had happened. I knew I needed to offer them some guidance.

We like to keep our children safe and happy and protected from the harmful realities of life, but that's an impossible task. People that children love get ill, have accidents, get divorced, or face other tragedies. Even when we think we are sheltering our children, they are often more aware of worrying events than we think they are. They're best served by straightforward, honest explanations. Otherwise, their imaginations can run to scenarios that are even more frightful than reality. As parents and teachers, sometimes the best thing we can do is set aside our well-planned agendas and have a discussion – even with preschoolers.

But how do we know what to say? We start by listening to children's comments and questions so that we know what they're worrying about. That way, we won't tell them more than they need to know, but we won't miss what truly worries them.

All communication has moral overtones, whether we're discussing major events (good or bad), or we're simply engaging in the back-and-forth of daily conversation. Those overtones come through in a variety of ways, the most important of which are *not* our words. Yes, the words we use are important, but they relay only a small part of what we communicate. Most of our communication is nonverbal. A classic study done by Albert Mehrabian, a professor at UCLA, revealed that only seven percent of what we communicate comes from our words. Our body language, gestures, facial expressions, and appearance make up fifty percent of what we communicate. Our "paralanguage" – the pitch, volume, tempo, and tone of our voice – conveys the rest.[1] If our words don't match our body language and paralanguage, it's not our words that children will "read."

Obviously, the bulk of our communication – body language and paralanguage – can't come through in texts. It takes place only when we're present. I know the nanny of an eight-year-old girl, who picks her up after school, takes her to piano lessons and birthday parties and sleepovers, supervises while her friends come and play, and stays with her until early evening when her mom gets home from work. So who is communicating moral principles to this young girl? Who are the significant adults in her life? The nanny certainly. Teachers. Mom and Dad. When does this communication happen? When these adults are present and the girl can watch them, listen to them, and interact with them.

Not only is it important to be physically present, but it's also important to be mentally and emotionally present. The first rule of communication is *listen*, and the first listener needs to be us. Patti Wood, a researcher on nonverbal communication, says, "I believe that the greatest gift we can give other people is to truly understand them, to really see them. And that one of the greatest feelings we can experience is that of being truly understood and seen."[2] Listening is a sign of respect, an indicator of morality. What's more, we must first listen before we can expect to be heard.

When it comes to listening to children and conversing with them, the earlier we begin, the better. I knew one dad who decided that his wife would best communicate with their two daughters from infancy through the elementary years. He planned to enter the loop when the girls neared adolescence and progressed through their teen years. When the girls were in college, he admitted to me that he had been wrong. He had not established a channel of communication when his daughters were young, and by adolescence, their focus had moved on to friends and mentors. They weren't interested in confiding in their dad. They still loved him, and he was influential in their lives, but he was not able to be the wise confidante that he had envisioned he would be. So begin good habits of communication when your children are young, and try to keep the channel open as they grow.

If you're a classroom teacher, establish good listening and conversation habits from the first time the children enter your classroom. Be there early, come prepared, and greet each child by name as they come through the door. Ask how they're doing. Maybe comment on a new haircut or new shoes or on the ballgame their team won (or lost) last week. Be interested in each of them. Care. That shows respect. It's basic morality.

In the classroom, conversation is often more structured, with the subject of the day's lesson providing a framework for discussions. At home, working together and playing together provide frameworks for conversation. Watch for opportunities to ask direct questions about moral issues, not in order to elicit a correct answer or create a teaching moment but to listen and learn as kids think out loud. Sometimes they need to talk to figure out what they think. So instead of using a discussion as a "teachable moment," use it as a "learnable moment" – and the learner is you.

For younger children, your questions might be as simple as, "What does it mean to be good? What does it mean to be generous? Do we always have to share? What does it mean to be fair to people?" Michele Borba suggests questions like, "What do tolerant people say and do? What do intolerant people say and do? What does it mean to be racist?" You know your kids. You often know the situations that are at the forefront of their minds. Tailor your discussions to their needs.

Listen for children's answers and thoughts. Don't presume to know what they think, feel, or will say. And when they've finished speaking, don't be too quick to respond. Count to ten if you need to. Sometimes when we leave a moment of silence before speaking, children will start talking again and will say something else that is deeper, more thoughtful, and even wiser than their first response.

Pausing also allows us to truly consider what children have said, which is *considerate* of us. It's good to reflect back to them what we heard them say. "You feel like it's unfair that you didn't get to go to the game with your big sister." If what we heard is right, the child feels like we listened. If what we heard is not quite right, she can correct us.

When we're ready to respond, it's helpful – especially with older kids – to ask, "May I add something here?" or "May I offer an insight?" If we establish a non-judgmental atmosphere that allows our children to safely air their thoughts and opinions, then they will most likely allow us the same safe space to respond with our thoughts and opinions. We give each other a chance to verbalize ideas, think through beliefs, come to solid conclusions, and grow wiser, even though we may not agree on every point. Writing about teens, Daniel J. Siegel says, "For both adolescent and adult, keeping the lines of communication open is the most basic principle of navigating these years well."[3]

Chapter 22
Screen Time, the Internet, and Social Media

"This time like all times is a very good one,
if we but know what to do with it."
– Ralph Waldo Emerson –

I grew up in a time of landline phones, no microwaves, and only three TV channels, all in black-and-white. Computers were huge banks of machines that filled entire rooms and were used only by the government and researchers. We never even imagined social media and video games. But my grandsons have known only an internet/social media culture. So they're fully immersed, while I only wade in it. All that to say, I'm no expert on screen time or social media. But one thing I know: no matter where we currently are technologically and no matter where we go from here, when it comes to the moral compass, True North does not change.

Of course, the internet and social media, as non-human entities, are neither moral nor immoral. They simply convey the content that people choose to post. That's where morality comes in. The internet offers access to an entire world of fact and falsehood, belief and opinion, information and disinformation, so if we choose to be part of it – and most of us do – we quickly find our morals involved.

David Brooks, in his book *The Road to Character*, points out three ways that the internet and social media have affected what he calls our "moral ecology." First, since we're bombarded with messages coming at us all day every day, "It's harder to attend to the soft, still voices that come from the depths." Those soft, still voices are often the ones that lead us into moral wisdom. Second, the thoughts that I share and the information I receive are tailored to my preferences. "Each individual can be the sun at the center of his or her own media solar system," says Brooks. Third, "[S]ocial media encourages a broadcasting personality . . . a hypercompetitive struggle for attention."[1]

Those last two points – being our own sun and competing for attention – deal with being self-centered, which is the lowest rung of the moral ladder. So what's the best way to grow and maintain moral wisdom in a world that's increasingly found online? To answer that question, we'll deal with two broad concerns: our influence on the internet and the internet's influence on us.

1) How our morality affects the internet.

Me affect the internet? That thought might be laughable. It's like thinking one drop of water can affect a whole lake. But each of us (including children) has a unique sphere of influence. We may be one "drop," but we cause ripples. Every time we're kind and respectful toward others, we nudge the world in the direction of kindness and respect. Even online. We're contributing to a better world.

Of course, we can also just as easily contribute to an uglier world. One aspect of the internet is the way it can let us feel anonymous or at least shielded by the physical distance between us and the readers of what we post. It can be easier to be impulsive and unkind to someone on social media than in person. That makes it easier to condemn people who disagree with us or have different beliefs. So we may need to remind our children – and ourselves – that the Golden Rule also applies online.

Discussions with kids about their online lives can provide more insight for us. Again, instead of using the discussion as a "teachable moment," we can use it as a "learnable moment." We can learn about our kids' viewpoints. Ask what respectful or disrespectful online experiences they've had – or have heard about from friends or other students. What made the experience respectful or not respectful? How would they suggest respecting others online? How would they suggest responding when others disrespect them online?

What we post often displays our values. I say *often* because online, we're never able to present ourselves as fully dimensional people. We present to the world the image that we want them to see of us. Teens, who are establishing their identity, are very conscious of crafting the image they want others to see online. But we adults do it too. Is that wrong? Is it okay? Can we avoid it, or is it just the nature of life online? Where's the line between presenting your best self and being deceptive? How much of your life is it safe to reveal? If you hide certain aspects of your life, are you being dishonest or wise? These are good questions to ponder with teens.

Jonathan Merritt, senior columnist for Religion News Service, suggests that bloggers should decide what they want the tone of their posts to convey, then choose three adjectives to describe that tone – for example: humorous, insightful, and friendly; or curious, gracious, and generous; or direct, challenging, and wise. He advises us to keep those three descriptions in mind each time we post so that we can consistently "be" those three for our readers. That's a good exercise for anyone who posts or texts, including kids. How do we want to affect people? What values do we want to show? What do we want people to feel when they see something we've posted (including photos)? We never know who is watching and listening, and we have more influence than we think. A single drop of water in a lake can make a difference, depending on what's in that drop.

2) How the internet affects our morality.

Years ago, George Gerbner, a researcher on the role of media in our culture, said, "Whoever tells the stories controls how the children grow up."[2] At that time, television told most of the stories. These days, most stories come to us online, and we have a much wider selection of what we choose to watch. In fact, the online world spreads quite a feast, offering us a healthy diet for our souls or an unhealthy one.

It's said that we are what we eat, and in a way, that's true. It has also been said that the same principle applies to our mental/moral diet as well. What we put into our bodies affects our health and so does what we put into our thoughts. Our minds will chew on it. It's what we will see in our dreams and what our thoughts will go to in our down time.

But it's not quite that simple. If we are what we see and hear, then we could simply sequester our children, shutting them off from history's tragedies and today's disturbing events, and they'd grow up morally wise. Yet that's not the case. Children raised in an overly protective environment actually grow up deficient in real life experience, which doesn't make them wise but leaves them ill-informed and ill-equipped to function in social settings outside their limited experience.

While it's important to be sensitive to which realities of life children are prepared to handle, we guide them toward moral wisdom by not being overly protective. Instead, we help them process what they see and hear. These days, children face harsh realities we wish they didn't have to deal with – active shooter drills in school, deportation of family members or friends, and much more. How do we help? First, by knowing the stages of development, we can be aware of what most children at each age are able to understand and process with the help of caring adults. Second, by listening to the specific children in our care, we can learn what they, in particular, understand or misunderstand. Then we can guide them toward a balanced view of real-life issues and help them grow toward compassion, respect, and moral wisdom.

But what we watch or read online is not the only issue with screens. Our other challenge is the amount of time we spend online. The all-encompassing online world is a relatively recent development. Abby Ohlheiser reported in the Washington Post that a May 2018 Pew Research Center study on teens and social media showed that 45% of teens are online almost constantly. She also found that "at this point, smartphone ownership [among teens] seems pretty universal even across different races and classes." As for computers at home, those with higher incomes are more likely to have them, while lower-income teens have less access.[3]

Research like this is fairly new, because only now are we able to collect data about a generation who grew up knowing only an online world. There is much yet to be learned and understood about the effects of screen time and social media on kids. Even so, researchers are giving us some helpful advice.

Guidelines published by the American Academy of Pediatrics suggest that we allow children in elementary school to spend only one hour a day with screen media. They recommend two hours a day for older kids. If you know kids who are stuck to a screen for a lot longer than that, you may be rolling your eyes at the AAP guidelines. You also may be wondering if those children are addicted to the screen.

I suspect that one of my grandsons would spend all day playing video games if his parents let him. Is he addicted? Dr. Rachel Kowert, author of *A Parent's Guide to Video Games*, says that there's nothing wrong with children loving to play video games as long as that's not their only leisure time activity. She says video game addiction is similar to a gambling addiction. To feel satisfied, the addict feels the need to play longer each time they come to the game, and it begins to affect every area of life.[4]

Anya Kamenetz, a reporter who specializes in education and technology, has written a book titled *The Art of Screen*

Time.[5] One of the experts she interviewed was Dr. Douglas Gentile from Iowa State University, who co-authored a study on screen media "addiction" in children. To ascertain whether or not a child is addicted, he asks questions like:

- Is their preferred media activity the only thing that puts them in a good mood?
- Are they angry or otherwise unhappy when forced to unplug?
- Is their use of screens increasing over time?
- Do they sneak around to use screens?
- Does it interfere with family activities, friendships, or school?

When we discuss screen time with our kids, the way we talk about it can affect how they respond. Dr. Michael Bishop, who runs a teen summer camp for "screen overuse," suggests that when we talk with children about overusing screen media, we refer to it as a "habit" rather than as an "addiction." "When teens think about their behavior as a habit," he says, "they are more empowered to change."[6]

Dr. Jenny Radetsky, the lead author of the AAP guidelines, recommends that families share screen time. In other words, watch movies or play games on screens together. Kamenetz says that her family's screen rules are "no media on weekdays," unplug at family dinner, and unplug before bedtime. Lauren Hale, a sleep researcher at Stony Brook University in New York, also has concerns about screen use and bedtime. She says that if we spend too much time on a screen too close to bedtime, it takes longer to fall asleep. Her family rules are: no screens within an hour before bedtime and no screens in the bedroom.[7]

What does screen time have to do with morality? Growing wise morally requires an apprenticeship in real life. We have to experience challenging situations face to face and shoulder to shoulder with a variety of people. That's the paradox of the internet's effect on us. On one hand, it can connect us with friends, family, or strangers. On the other hand, it can disconnect us from face to face communication.

Our online culture also allows us to narrow our contacts to only people who are like us or people in "our tribe." When we narrow those contacts, we limit the opportunity to seriously consider the viewpoints of people who are not like us. It becomes easy to ignore challenging truths that we'd rather not face, even though those truths would help us grow toward moral maturity. We limit our opportunities to grow and exercise our moral muscles.

There's another issue that I believe is at least partly related to screen time: loneliness. The United Kingdom has recently recognized loneliness as a major, widespread problem and has appointed a "minister of loneliness" to help address it. Some people are wondering if the U.S. needs to deal with the growing problem of loneliness as well. Christine A. Padesky, a clinical psychologist, says, "Loneliness doesn't mean lack of contact with people. It has nothing to do with how many people you interact with in a day. It has more to do with the perception that your social needs are not being met, that you don't feel meaningful connections or acceptance."[8] That can happen whether we're online or off-line, but it's strange that with the internet, we're more connected than ever, yet we're lonelier than ever. It's something to think about. It's also a reason to make sure kids have real, face to face connections with a variety of people.

The truth is that all the practices of moral wisdom – responsibility, empathy, self-control, generosity, honesty, gratitude, patience, humility, kindness, and love – can be exercised online, and should be. But exercising these online is necessarily limited, and it's a different experience from being empathetic, self-controlled, generous, honest, and kind in person.

When it comes to screen time, whatever limits you set, try to set them when children are young, stay within those limits yourself, and be flexible. As kids grow older, let them help create reasonable limits for the family or classroom. Anya Kamenetz may have the best advice: "Enjoy screens. Not too much. Mostly together."

Chapter 23
Why Children Choose the Wrong Path

"There are bugs in our souls that lead us
toward selfishness and pride,
that tempt us to put lower loves over higher loves."
– David Brooks, *The Road to Character* –

Growing wise morally means learning to take responsibility for ourselves and our choices. We learn to 1) face the fact that we made a wrong choice and admit it, 2) take responsibility for the consequences, and 3) change our choices and habits to healthier ones.

When we've made a wrong moral choice, we've sinned. We don't often use the word *sin*, perhaps because it carries so much weight and sounds so ominous. But everyone talks about sin all the time. We simply use different words to describe it. We talk about sin when we expose injustice and demand justice. We address sin when we confront wrongs and insist that they be righted, when we raise an outcry over public leaders who lie or bully or embezzle or cheat, and when we expect consequences for genocide, kidnapping, and child abuse. Every day, the news presents us with all kinds of people talking about all kinds of sin but not calling it sin. And that's okay, because it's not what we call it that's important. What's important is that we recognize it as wrong and stand against it both in society and in our own personal lives.

The Greek word that Luke uses for *sin* in the Lord's Prayer is *hamartia*, which means *missing the mark* or *missing the target*. I like to think of sin as *missing the mark*, because that implies that there's a goal. It also suggests that when we miss it, we can try again. In archery, the bull's eye is the mark. For morality, what's the mark? Acting toward others the way we want them to act toward us (Matthew 7:12, Luke 6:31). In other words, respect.

But why do we miss the mark in the first place? Why would anyone be irresponsible, uncaring, undisciplined, greedy, dishonest, ungrateful, impatient, self-glorifying, rude, or hateful. (You can come up with plenty of other descriptors. I've simply listed here the opposite of my ten essential signs of moral wisdom.) We rarely get up in the morning thinking, "I'm going to be ungrateful and rude today." So maybe it's as simple as not knowing where the bull's-eye is.

But there are other reasons that we – and children – might miss the mark. I've listed several below. Note that these reasons do not excuse responsibility for bad behavior, but they do help us 1) understand children and what they are struggling with and 2) address not just the misbehavior but the underlying source of it, the way we try to treat not just the symptoms of an illness but the source of the infection.

Here are some possible reasons for why children might miss the mark.

1. Lack of knowledge or skills needed to navigate life challenges

If children are taught that the bull's-eye is to get ahead and be better than the next guy, then they've been given the wrong knowledge. If they've never been taught to how to share or think of the other person, then they may lack the skills to get along with others and make wise moral choices. So when children make the wrong choice, ask yourself if they know the right choice. Have they been taught the skills to handle this issue?

2. Physical or emotional stress

We and our children may know what the right behavior is, and we may have the skills, but if we're worn-out physically or emotionally, we may not push ourselves to do what we know. If we're tired or hungry or getting sick or in pain (physically or emotionally), we're more likely to be cranky, disagreeable, and downright obstinate. We may revert to immature ways of relating to others. So when children make the wrong choice, ask yourself if they could be tired, hungry, or sick.

3. Frustration

We get frustrated when something blocks our path or obstructs our efforts. Frustration pushes us to the limits of our patience. At that point, a nudge can send us over the line. So when children make the wrong choice, look to see if they were frustrated in some way. Was the activity too difficult, too advanced for them? Have they been trying to tell you something, but you weren't listening? Have they been trying to do a project with inadequate tools or poor directions?

4. Power

In a world as competitive as ours, the temptation is great to get ahead and gain advantage in ways that are either questionable or blatantly wrong. The old adage that power corrupts is often true. It takes a strong person to lead without being corrupted. So when children make the wrong choice, ask yourself whether they might be trying to gain the upper hand or to hold on to a position of power.

5. The need for acceptance

Sometimes children do things they know are wrong in order to impress a certain person or group, or to avoid being embarrassed in front of classmates and friends who are taking the wrong path. Kids may "go along" out of the need to protect themselves or someone else from ridicule or harm. They may actively do wrong or turn a blind eye to others who are doing wrong in order not to rock the boat. So when children make the wrong choice, ask yourself if they might be trying to gain or preserve the acceptance of certain people.

6. Fear

We may choose to do wrong because we fear losing what we have – possessions, influence, lifestyle, position, opportunity. Getting a new brother or sister, moving to a new school, and other life changes often make us afraid that we're going to lose out, and we may miss the mark in the way we react. So when children make the wrong choice, ask if they might be trying to maintain the status quo. What are they afraid of losing?

7. Stress

When we're stressed, we tend to revert to more immature ways of coping. Richard E. Nelson and Judith C. Galas, authors of *The Power to Prevent Suicide: A Guide for Teens Helping Teens*, list forty powerful stressors that can trigger teens to make the wrong choice. Among them are the obvious (the death of a parent or friend, divorce or separation of parents, breakup of a significant friendship) as well as the less obvious (a new sibling, a stay-at-home parent starting work full-time, beginning a new sport or activity, even winning an award or going on vacation or to camp).[1] While these stressors can be factors in suicide, more often they're factors in pressuring kids to make other wrong choices. When kids do make wrong choices, see if they might be experiencing stress.

As a reminder: These reasons do not excuse bad behavior. They do help us understand and empathize. They also help us figure out the best way to address the behavior.

The prophet Isaiah wrote that our sins separate us from God (Isaiah 59:2). Since we hold *imago dei* within us, whenever we miss the mark by what we think, say, or do, we suppress the image of God in us. We distance ourselves. And not only from God. Disrespecting others separates us from them. Disrespecting the earth God created separates us from nature. We miss out on the best of what life can be. So the goal of dealing with sin (missing the mark) is to close the great rift between us and others, between us and nature, between us and God, and even the rift within ourselves.

Closing the rift requires *repentance*, another semi-obscure word used mostly in church. My favorite definition of repentance comes from Welsh minister and writer Selwyn Hughes.[2] He says that repentance is changing our minds about where true life is found. True life is not found in greed but in gratitude, not in hubris but in humility, not in condemnation but in grace, not in lust but in love. When we change our minds about where true life is found, we can recalibrate our moral compass toward True North and head once again in the direction of life.

Chapter 24
Correcting the Course

"In one mile, turn right. Stay in the right lane."
Siri

The calm voice of the GPS is familiar to many of us, directing us to our destination, although I've been calmly led to the wrong street more than once. Still, Siri is right most of the time, and when we take the wrong exit or pass up the right one, she can usually get us back on course from wherever we are. We hope our children's conscience becomes a dependable moral GPS system, able to direct them down the right path and get them back on course when they take a wrong turn.

We and our children need to see our wrongs as right-able, our cracks as repairable. We need to see our relationships with God, others, self, and nature as restorable. The desire for reparation, restoration, justice, and accountability – moral reciprocity – is built into human nature (although we tend to demand it for others and evade it for ourselves). So . . . justice? Yes. Accountability? Yes. Reparation? Yes.

What about mercy? Yes, that, too. In those who are morally wise, mercy exists side by side with justice (which Tony Campolo says "is nothing more than love transformed into social policy"). Amy Engel, an author and former criminal defense attorney, strikes a balance between mercy and justice by differentiating between "moral complexity" and "moral flexibility." She agrees that there are definite moral lines beyond which we should not go. That is not flexible. However, she believes that we should also take into consideration "moral complexity." She says, "I believe it is entirely possible to recognize the humanity in others, to try to understand why they do what they do, to even feel some sense of pain for them, and still believe they have crossed a moral line that can never be uncrossed. For me, none of those ideas negates the others."[1]

So what's the best way to deal with missing the mark? It depends. One thing is certain: If we adults want to respond wisely, our frame of mind is crucial. Often our first reaction is anger or exasperation. Dr. Stanley Turecki, author of *The Difficult Child*, suggests that parents and teachers not allow themselves to be drawn into the child's turmoil.[2] In other words, don't take it personally. Step back, detach, try to think clearly and respond calmly. (Of course, that's much easier said than done.)

In the face of a challenge, my father often says, "You can see it as a problem, or you can see it as an opportunity." If we look at behavior challenges as opportunities instead of problems, we have a better chance of bringing about positive change. When kids miss the mark, we have a real-life opportunity to help them learn how to handle their problems, to think through cause and effect, and to consider other perspectives – in short, to help them find their moral compass. So instead of simply trying to eliminate negative behavior, we work with children to help them understand that certain behaviors ultimately don't work. They harm others and/or ourselves and don't make for a better world.

When we looked at the stages of development, we noted two basic principles that are foundational to morality: 1) cause and effect, and 2) perspective-taking. Children begin learning cause and effect as soon as they're born. Perspective-taking kicks in around age two. But we humans seem to need a lifetime of practice in these two principles. We constantly underestimate or overlook the effects that our moral choices have on others, and we often fail to see from the other person's perspective or "walk a mile in their shoes" as the saying goes. The process of growing morally wise takes a lifetime. So as we help children change course, we can expect to find ourselves guiding them again and again to consider other perspectives and think through cause/effect. This is discipline, which literally means training.

It's important to try to strike a balance between parent-centered discipline (authoritarian) and child-centric responses (permissive). In a permissive atmosphere, the child has no reason to stop, attend, and process cause/effect or to consider perspective-taking. On the opposite side of the scale is authoritarian discipline, which relies on the assertion of parental power or the withdrawal of love. Under authoritarian discipline, children focus on protecting themselves, which turns their attention away from others and the perspective-taking process.

Most parents fall somewhere in between authoritarian and permissive. What's most important is that children understand that we love them. It's also important to be as consistent as we can, so that whether our parenting style is stricter or more lenient, our children know what is expected of them and what consequences might be imposed for wrong choices. When we do impose consequences, it's best to make sure that the consequences fit the infraction as much as possible.

Time Out is an appropriate first step in almost every situation and can be valuable not only for the child but for us as well. The practice of Time Out was originally intended to remove children from the troublesome situation so they could calm down and think. It allows *us* to calm down and think as well. Researcher John C. Gibbs says, "[T]he time-out consequence works best when it is framed in moral or social perspective-taking terms (the sequestered child is reminded in clear, simple terms of why their act was wrong or harmful, and a 'sorry' is elicited and accepted . . .)."[3]

How long should a Time Out be? Gauge it by the age of the child. If she's two, two minutes is about the limit. If he's four, four minutes. Eight, eight minutes. Gibbs suggests that when children are older, the Time Out chair could be called a "reflection chair," a place for them to reflect on what happened. When the child is even older, the place of reflection becomes a couch where, after the set time for reflection, the adult joins the child to discuss the situation. Whatever the age of the child and wherever Time Out occurs, when time is up, the adult needs to talk with the child about what happened and come up with a plan – and hopefully an apology, which may need to be expressed by both adult and child.

Here are some tips, eight E's, to help you discuss what went wrong and to help children find their moral compass again.

1. **Empathize** with the one who was hurt. If this is a situation in which someone was hurt (physically or emotionally), instead of turning your full attention to the wrongdoer, turn first to the one who was hurt and express concern. This is assuming that the wrongdoing has stopped and no one is in danger (including the wrongdoer). If the wrongdoer wanted the attention, then he's not rewarded for what he did to get it. But even if the action wasn't attention-seeking, turning your attention first to the one who was hurt models the empathy and perspective-taking that children need to see and emulate.

2. **Eye to eye**, heart to heart, privately if possible. We touched on eye-to-eye and heart-to-heart when we looked at communication. When the discussion deals with behavior management, it's best to have the conversation in private. Then the child can respond more sincerely and not be swayed by whoever might be listening or watching. Respecting a child's need for privacy also avoids embarrassing the child in front of others.

3. **Ears open.** Avoid asking, "Why did you do that?" even though that's one thing we're trying to figure out. When put on the spot to explain themselves, even adults often don't know why, in that moment, they made a wrong choice. "Why" can also put children immediately on the defensive. Instead, we can ask, "What happened?" Then we need to listen. After the child stops speaking, it's best to stay silent for a few seconds. The child may have another thought to express, and the silence

may draw it out. Besides, we need a silent moment to seriously consider what has been said and how we will respond.

4. **Explain** why the behavior was wrong. Better yet, ask the child to explain why it was wrong and why it misses the mark. We looked at the whys of moral wisdom in an earlier chapter. Focus on health and safety and the way life works best.

5. **Express** disappointment. For young children, a simple, "I'm sad that you chose to hit instead of using your words" can be enough. For older children, it may be more effective to say something like, "You're usually such a thoughtful person. I'm disappointed at the careless words and tone of voice you used with your cousin."

6. **Expect** the best. Assure the child that you have confidence in him and believe that he'll make a better choice next time. This, of course, assumes that the child is aware of a better choice. So . . .

7. **Explore** with the child how she might plan to handle the situation next time. Show her a better way. If she has thrown her shoe out of frustration over a stubborn knot, we can teach her – or remind her – that when we're frustrated, we can ask for help, or we can set the problem aside and go back to it later when we've calmed down. We can use the "HALF it" practice to calm ourselves: Hands relax, Abdomen relax, Lungs breathe deeply, Face relax. Repeat. In other words, we can

equip children with real life skills that will make life better for everyone.

8. **Encourage** the child to think of ways to make the situation right. That may include apologizing, putting things to right as best he can, and making reparations if necessary.

As we help children grow toward moral wisdom, it's important to give them hope and a positive way of looking at the moral issues they struggle with. According to Richard Rohr and Andreas Ebert, "[o]ur 'sins,' in fact, are the other side of our gift."[4] Their book *The Enneagram* explains this further, but to put it simply, our gifts can easily become our sins. Persistence that has missed the mark can turn into stubbornness. Compassion can become pity and condescension. Leadership flips to tyranny, confidence to hubris. Our strength is our weakness. "But if we . . . do not struggle against the weaknesses in ourselves," writes David Brooks, "then we will gradually spoil some core piece of ourselves."[5]

The journey to maturity is slow going and always will be. Those who are wise have learned to travel with their shadow self, but they continue to try to flip the coin, turning their weaknesses into strengths, standing back up when they fall, and trying again whenever they miss the mark. We can encourage children to do the same.

Chapter 25
True North

"Eventually kids become grownups too,
and from there, the world is whatever they choose to make it."
– Allison Winn Scotch –

There is a hub around which all the moral life of the world revolves. This hub has always existed and always will. It's the True North that our moral compass points to. Ignore it, and we fly off in dangerous directions. But fix our heart on it, and we have an accurate, reliable inner moral compass that will never fail. What is this hub, this True North?

Love.

Gracious, self-giving, unconditional love is our True North. No matter where we are, no matter when, no matter what situation we're in, we can look to love as our guide, because God is love. Love is always open for business, and it's available to anyone and everyone. In fact, our one purpose in life is to learn and practice love. Anyone can do it.

Are you old? Learn and practice love.

Are you young? Learn and practice love.

Are you rich? Learn and practice love.

Are you poor? Learn and practice love.

Are you healthy? Learn and practice love.

Are you sick? Learn and practice love.

Are you educated? Learn and practice love.

Are you uneducated? Learn and practice love.

Love, said Jesus, is the greatest commandment. "First, love the Lord your God with all your heart and mind and strength," he said. "Second, love your neighbor as yourself" (Mark 12:29-31, Matthew 22:37-40). According to Mark, Jesus's next words were, "There is no commandment greater than these." Why? Because love has it all covered. If we love, we don't need to be told to honor our father and mother. Love takes care of that. If we love, we don't need to be told to respect our neighbors and not covet what's theirs. Love covers that. If we love, we don't need to be told not to lie or steal or denigrate people. Love wouldn't do that. As the apostle Paul said, "Love does no harm to its neighbor. Therefore love is the fulfillment of the law" (Romans 13:10, NIV).

Our ancient scriptures tell us that in one of God's first conversations with Abraham, God said, "I will bless you . . . and you will be a blessing" (Genesis 12:2, NIV). That promise is the bedrock of our morality. God blesses us with gracious, merciful love, so we can bless others with gracious, merciful love. And who are these others? They are people who are like and unlike us, who are of our "tribe" and not of our "tribe."

We are to treat everyone with grace and respect, not only for their sakes but for ours as well. When we close our eyes, cloister our hearts, and exclude individuals or groups from our loving-kindness, we diminish ourselves and our own humanity. We contribute to the disintegration of an already fragmented world, which then makes *us* feel fragmented. But when we integrate love, peace, grace, and respect into our dealings with

all people, we contribute to mending the world and making it
whole, which in turn gives us a sense of wholeness.

This is the moral compass we want to pass on to our
children, this compass that points toward love as its True
North. But here's the twist: sometimes it's our children who
bring *us* back to our moral compass, our True North. Christian
Bales, a 2018 graduating senior, said in his valedictory speech,
"There's a misguided notion that wisdom is directly
proportional to age, but we're disproving that daily. Sometimes
the wisest are the youngest in our lives, the ones who haven't yet
been desensitized to the atrocities of our world."¹ Remember the
tale of "The Emperor's New Clothes"? It was the young child
who pointed out that the emperor had no clothes on. God gives
us children to grow us up.

We and our children are on the journey to moral
wisdom together, helping each other, learning from each other.
And the journey is not a short one. It's a lifelong process. Often
when I think I've got one virtue down, I experience something
that reveals a new aspect of that virtue – and of my lack – and I
realize that there's more growth ahead.

So I want to reiterate that morality is not a one-and-
done lesson. We can't teach sharing to four-year-olds and expect
them to share from that moment on. We can't teach character
versus image to teens and expect them to embrace character
overnight. We can't talk to adults about hypocrisy and expect us
to automatically root all hypocrisy out of our lives. We can't even
talk to ourselves about gracious love and expect that we'll never
again have to struggle with finding grace and love in our heart
for others. Still, when we know that our moral compass points

to love, we can know where we're supposed to be headed and adjust our course accordingly. We can try to make the most loving choices.

The more we learn about selfless love and the more we practice it, the more we will see how expansive it is. Love contains everything we could ever want: hope, joy, peace, courage, and everything that makes life good. Love is unlimited in its reach. It has no borders. It flows past, around, over, and through all boundaries and divisions that we humans can construct. Love is one of the great wonders of the world.

So choose the path of love. You are the one who will make a difference in children's lives. Head toward love. Always. It's our True North. Stand on love. Lean your full weight on love, for love never fails. Love is your help. Love is your health. Love is your hope. Love is your home. Live in love.

Gift children with this moral compass. Together we can love the world into being a better place.

End Notes

Chapter 1

[1] Barbara O'Neal, blog post, http://writerunboxed.com/2017/04/26/the-complex-power-of-mapping-the-world-of-your-novel/

[2] "By more than two-to-one (68% to 25%), white evangelical Protestants say the U.S. does not have a responsibility to accept refugees." http://www.pewresearch.org/fact-tank/2018/05/24/republicans-turn-more-negative-toward-refugees-as-number-admitted-to-u-s-plummets/

[3] Michael Gerson, "The Trump Evangelicals Have Lost Their Gag Reflex," *The Washington Post*, Jan. 22, 2018.

[4] Fred Rogers, *The Mister Rogers Parenting Book* (Philadelphia: Running Press, 2002).

[5] Robert Coles, *The Moral Intelligence of Children* (NY: Plume, 1998).

[6] Neil Postman, *The Disappearance of Childhood* (NY: Vintage/Random House, 1994).

Chapter 2:

[1] Robert Coles, *The Moral Intelligence of Children*, (NY: Plume, 1998).

[2] William Cantwell Smith, quoted in James W. Fowler, *Stages of Faith* (NY: HarperOne, 1981).

[3] Michele Borba, *Building Moral Intelligence* (San Francisco: Jossey-Bass, 2002).

[4] John C. Gibbs, *Moral Development and Reality* (NY: Allyn and Bacon, 2010).

[5] Plato, *Laws*, Book XI (Oxford, UK: Acheron Press, 2012).

[6] Karyn Henley, *Child-Sensitive Teaching* (Nashville, TN: Child Sensitive Communication, 2008 ed).

[7] Scott Spencer as interviewed by Terri Gross on *Fresh Air*, National Public Radio, March 19, 2008.

Chapter 3

[1] Erik H. Erikson, *Childhood and Society* (NY: W.W. Norton, 1963).

[2] Jean Piaget quoted by Dorothy G. Singer and Tracey A. Revenson in *A Piaget Primer: How a Child Thinks* (NY: Penguin, 1978).

[3] James W. Fowler, *Stages of Faith: The Psychology of Human De-velopment and the Quest for Meaning* (San Francisco: Harper, 1981).

[4] John C. Gibbs, *Moral Development and Reality* (NY: Allyn and Bacon, 2010).

Chapter 4

[1] James W. Fowler, *Stages of Faith: The Psychology of Human Development and the Quest for Meaning* (San Francisco: Harper, 1981).

[2] Thomas Lickona, *Raising Good Children* (NY: Bantam, 1983).

[3] Marguerite Wright, *I'm Chocolate, You're Vanilla: Raising Healthy Black and Biracial Children in a Race-Conscious World* (San Francisco: Jossey-Bass, 2000).

Chapter 5

[1] Howard Gardner, *The Unschooled Mind* (NY: HarperCollins, 1991).

[2] John C. Gibbs, *Moral Development and Reality* (NY: Allyn and Bacon, 2010).

[3] Robert Solomon, tape series *No Excuses: Existentialism and the Meaning of Life* (Chantilly, VA: Teaching Company, 2000).

[4] Michele Borba, *Building Moral Intelligence* (San Francisco: Jossey-Bass, 2002).

Chapter 6

[1] Howard Gardner, *The Unschooled Mind* (NY: HarperCollins, 1991).

Chapter 7

[1] Daniel J. Siegel, *Brainstorm: The Power and Purpose of the Teenage Brain* (NY: Tarcher Perigee, 2015).

[2] Daniel Goleman, interview in *What We Believe but Cannot Prove*, ed. John Brockman (NY: Harper, 2006).

Chapter 8

[1] David Kupelian, "Selling Sex and Corruption to Your Kids" <www.worldnetdaily.com/news/article.asp?ARTICLE_ID=3 6598> accessed 10/01/08.

[2] Anastasia Goodstein of Ypulse, as quoted in "Teens Give Out MySpace Pages," *USA Today*, Monday, January 9, 2006.

[3] Juliet Schor, *Born to Buy: The Commercialized Child and the New Consumer Culture* (NY: Scribner, 2005).

[4] Kevin Huggins, *Parenting Adolescents* (Colorado Springs: Navpress, 1989).

[5] Orson Scott Card, introduction to *Speaker for the Dead* (NY: Tor, 1991).

Chapter 9

[1] John C. Gibbs, *Moral Development and Reality* (NY: Allyn and Bacon, 2010).

[2] N. Kenneth Rideout, *The Truth You Know You Know* (Nashville, TN: NDX Press, 2005).

Chapter 10

[1] Michele Borba, *Building Moral Intelligence* (San Francisco: Jossey-Bass, 2002).

[2] Simone Pétrement, *Simone Weil: A Life* (NY: Pantheon, 1976).

[3] Brené Brown, *Rising Strong* (NY: Random House, 2015).

[4] Diana Butler Bass, *Grateful: The Transformative Power of Giving Thanks* (San Francisco: HarperOne, 2018).

[5] Barnaby Conrad and Monte Schulz, eds., *Snoopy's Guide to the Writing Life* (Cincinnati, OH: Writer's Digest Books, 2002).

[6] Madeleine Albright in an interview on Public Radio International's *The World*, 4.25.18.

[7] Eleanor Roosevelt, *The Book of Common Sense Etiquette* (np: Open Road Media, 2016).

[8] Father Thomas Hopko, "Living in Communion," *Communion*, Orthodox Peace Fellowship, The Netherlands, 2/1/95.

[9] Krista Tippett, *Becoming Wise* (NY: Penguin, 2016).

[10] Becca Stevens, *Love Heals* (Nashville, TN: Thomas Nelson, 2017).

Chapter 15

[1] David Brooks, *The Road to Character* (NY: Random House, 2016).

[2] http://time.com/money/5244916/tammie-jo-shults-southwest-pilot/

Chapter 17

[1] Daniel J. Siegel, *Brainstorm: The Power and Purpose of the Teenage Brain* (NY: Tarcher Perigee, 2015).

Chapter 18

[1] John C. Gibbs, *Moral Development and Reality* (NY: Allyn and Bacon, 2010).

[2] Timothy Keller, *The Reason for God* (NY: Dutton, 2008).

[3] Katherine Boo, *Behind the Beautiful Forevers* (NY: Random House, 2014).

Chapter 19

[1] Thomas Lickona, *Raising Good Children* (NY: Bantam, 1983).

[2] Sara Bullard, *Teaching Tolerance* (NY: Doubleday, 1997).

Chapter 20

[1] David Brooks, *The Road to Character* (NY: Random House, 2016).

Chapter 21

[1] Quoted by Patti Wood in *Snap* (Novato, CA: New World Library, 2012).

[2] Ibid.

[3] Daniel J. Siegel, *Brainstorm: The Power and Purpose of the Teenage Brain* (NY: Tarcher Perigee, 2015).

Chapter 22

[1] David Brooks, *The Road to Character* (NY: Random House, 2016).

[2] George Gerbner, Speech. 1990 National Congress on Storytelling.

[3] Abby Ohlheiser, "45% of Teens are Online Almost Constantly," Washington Post online, June 1, 2018.

[4] Dr. Rachel Kowert, interviewed by Annie Fox for familyconfidential.com 3/13/18 "Good News About Kids and Video Games: Dr. Rachel Kowert."

[5] Anya Kamenetz, "What the Screen Time Experts Do with Their Own Kids," interview on nprEd, February 6, 2018. https://www.npr.org/sections/ed/2018/02/06/579555110/what-the-screen-time-experts-do-with-their-own-kids

[6] As quoted by Anya Kamenetz in "Screen Addiction Among Teens: Is There Such a Thing?" nprEd, February 5, 2018. https://www.npr.org/sections/ed/2018/02/05/579554273/screen-addiction-among-teens-is-there-such-a-thing

[7] Jenny Radetsky and Lauren Hale quoted by Anya Kamenetz, "What the Screen Time Experts Do with Their Own Kids," interview on nprEd, February 6, 2018. https://www.npr.org/sections/ed/2018/02/06/579555110/what-the-screen-time-experts-do-with-their-own-kids

[8] Christine A. Padesky, quoted by David Levine, U.S. News and World Report, April 27, 2018. https://health.usnews.com/health-care/patient-advice/articles/2018-04-27/the-uk-now-has-a-minister-of-loneliness-does-the-us-need-one

Chapter 23

---

[1] Richard E. Nelson and Judith C. Galas, *The Power to Prevent Suicide: A Guide for Teens Helping Teens* (Minneapolis: Free Spirit Publishing, 2006).

[2] Selwyn Hughes, *Christ Empowered Living* (Farnham, Surrey, England: Crusade for World Revival, 1998).

Chapter 24

[1] Amy Engel, "Seeing Both Sides," *Publishers Weekly*, March 6, 2017.

[2] Stanley Turecki, *The Difficult Child* (NY: Bantam, 2000).

[3] John C. Gibbs, *Moral Development and Reality* (NY: Allyn and Bacon, 2010).

[4] Richard Rohr and Andreas Ebert, *The Enneagram* (NY: Crossroad, 2011).

[5] David Brooks, *The Road to Character* (NY: Random House, 2016).

Chapter 25

[1] Christian Bales valedictory speech: https://abcnews.go.com/US/valedictorians-speech-barred-political-gave-bullhorn/story?id=55469094

Made in the USA
Middletown, DE
15 November 2018